# SIMPLY ELEGANT COUNTRY FOODS

Copyright © 1986 by Carol Lowe-Clay

All rights reserved.
No portion of this book may be reproduced—
mechanically, electronically or by any other
means, including photocopying—without
written permission of the publisher.

**Library of Congress**
**Cataloging in Publication Data**

Lowe-Clay, Carol.
  Simply elegant country foods.

  Includes index.
  1. Cookery, American. I. Title.
TX715.L9104  1986          641.5          86-4046
ISBN 0-913589-20-9

Cover and interior design: Trezzo-Braren Studio
Cover photograph: Langdon Clay
Typography: Villanti & Sons, Printers, Inc.
Printing: Capital City Press

Williamson Publishing Co.
Charlotte, Vermont 05445

Manufactured in the United States of America

10   9   8   7   6   5   4   3   2

# SIMPLY ELEGANT COUNTRY FOODS

## Downhome Goes Uptown

### Carol Lowe~Clay

design and illustrations by Loretta Trezzo

**WILLIAMSON PUBLISHING**
CHARLOTTE, VERMONT 05445

To Owen, for all the reasons . . .

## Acknowledgements

Many thanks to—

Wild Farm for its recipes and style, and
to Ann who generously shares it all.

Slater and Davy for their sophisticated
little palates, and their enthusiastic critiques
of these recipes.

The many people, family, and friends who
willingly gave their recipes and ideas to this
book.

And to Susan for her encouragement and
support all along.

# Contents

# Preface

Some of the most delightful and surprising meals spring forth from an almost-bare larder, yet often, overstocked shelves produce meals of boring predictability. That empty larder, I suspect, allows us a "come what may" attitude. In that abandon, we relax and allow ourselves the freedom to create.

Knowledge of classic cooking and basic technique not only increases skills but also gives confidence. This confidence enables us to lighten the rules, and feel the spontaneity that gives joy in the kitchen.

Disciplined cooking styles and restrictive stereotypes have given way to a relaxed blending of technique. We can take what we want from classic and nouvelle schools or from cuisines around the world. We cherish fresh local food as well as search out intriguing ingredients from afar.

We take the best of what we grew up with—the comforting tastes and traditional combinations—and develop them in new ways.

We feel a wholesome freshness in the immediacy of summer cooking, a decadent richness to our desserts, a zestiness in grilled meats with fruit, a warming familiarity with old favorites. The integrating factor is trusting our own judgements and personal balances.

7

Recipes give form to cooking: when used correctly, they are but guidelines to combinations and preparations. They suggest the desired balance, but they don't prescribe. Only you know what is in your larder, or that your garden is wild with parsley. The recipes within serve as incentives, starting points for you to venture forth. Feel free to substitute or add to your heart's and mind's delight. Unexpected pleasures lay in wait.

Your meals can be gutsy or refined, spontaneous or planned, in the kitchen or in an unexpected setting. There can be contrast and contradiction in every aspect of the meal. Choose from simple spontaneous preparations (based perhaps on a sprig of watercress from a walk along a stream) or formal menus that take days of preparation: chocolate mousse cake on Sunday followed by brown rice and vegetables on Monday. A meal might unite varied regional specialties: a French leek and potato soup, Greek grilled fish with corn bread, and maple mousse for dessert. Sterling with wicker, or linen and ribbons, formal dinners in a hay field—all give us license to develop our own styles.

Simple presentations are often the most elegant. I think of the bright green of tender new asparagus, served on a plain white platter —to me far more lovely than a fussy sauced vegetable. Fussy is not necessarily elegant, trendy may not be as good, classic may not be as healthy, simply can be most elegant.

Complexity is no longer the standard of superiority. Freshness and character, however, may be. Local cheese on freshly made whole grain bread with flavored mayonnaise has much value in its honesty. Likewise, the uncomplicated taste of sun-warmed tomatoes is a definite gastronomic high point.

For me and for my family it is the little moments that we share, the style we nurture, the pauses to wonder and refresh that give our lives richness and build our heritage. It is our traditions that define our days and give us the memories we carry forth with us.

Hannukah, Christmas and Solstice are all celebrated at our house, the more celebrating the better. A lapse in our own holidays and we borrow from other cultures and weave a delicate balance of tradition and hope. We toast, light candles, feast; we are thankful for harvests, for lengthening days, for each other. A birthday, anniversary, momentous occasions, or a thunderstorm, apple blossoms, a walk in the dark—all can inspire us to cheer. Creating our own celebrations adds joy and appreciation to our every day.

Food itself often inspires festivities. One recent Saturday evening, I began preparing a coffee cake. The yeasty aromas gave warmth to our evening; we all went to bed with anticipation of the morning's treat. Next morning, the baking aromas awakened us to great excitement. A child, unprompted, set the table, pouring grapefruit juice in wine glasses. We heated milk and made *cafe au lait*. I discovered leftover birthday candles and put one in the cake for each person. We blew them out, sharing wishes. A special morning evolved from this impromptu baking; being unexpected made it more special still.

Eat in new places: have tea in the study, dessert by the fire, supper along a riverbend. Use props: curling ribbon and flowers hanging from ceiling lights, balloons from trees, candles in walnut shells floating down a river . . . meals become events. The table becomes the stage, our private and everchanging still-life, our gathering place.

On an incredibly gorgeous June day during haying, I happened upon a large patch of brilliant red, wild strawberries. The children and I fell right down to the obvious task of eating. We took handfuls home and made tiny little strawberry soufflés, befitting the berries' size. This spontaneous celebration has become a yearly event. We live somewhere else now, but this repeated ritual connects us to that beautiful day in a field and a time gone by.

The world is yours to create in, and, in a small way, is yours to create.

# Sweet Breads, Muffins & Coffee Cakes

# A POT OF TEA AND SWEET CREAM SCONES

*"There are few hours in life more agreeable
than the hour dedicated to the ceremony known as afternoon tea."*
HENRY JAMES

In my house, we do not take tea nearly often enough, but whenever we do, we vow to make it a more frequent ritual. It calms us and focuses us, a quiet time together away from the business of our days. Owen best likes Hu Kwa Tea; the rest of us mostly like the idea and almost any loose tea will do. Truly, take the time to brew a potful instead of using tea bags. It certainly adds to those feelings of specialness, as well as to the flavor. Besides, teapots are so pretty and cheering on a gray afternoon.

1. Bring out a favorite china teapot. Pour hot water into it and let stand to warm the pot.
2. Meanwhile, measure the required amount of water for tea, and bring to a boil in a kettle.
3. As water comes close to boil, empty the teapot of standing water. Add 1 teaspoon of loose tea per cup plus one for the pot.
4. Fill the pot with *just* boiling water and let it steep for 5 minutes (no longer—the tea becomes bitter).
5. Serve with lemon or milk. Have an additional pot of hot water ready to dilute the tea if desired.

# SWEET CREAM SCONES

With tea, most days, we have toast with butter and honey, but on special days, we make these Sweet Cream Scones. Spread a white tablecloth, place flowers on the table, and feel the transformation, in your day, in yourself.

| | |
|---|---|
| 1⅔ | cups flour (2 cups white flour, total, may be used instead of ⅓ cup whole wheat flour) |
| ⅓ | cup whole wheat flour |
| 1 | tablespoon baking powder |
| 2 | tablespoons granulated sugar |
| ½ | teaspoon salt |
| ¼ | cup butter, preferably sweet butter |
| 2 | eggs |
| ⅓ | cup heavy cream |
| 2 | teaspoons granulated sugar |

1. Preheat oven to 400 degrees.
2. Combine flour, baking powder, 2 tablespoons sugar, and salt.
3. Cut in the butter with 2 knives until the mixture is well combined, and resembles coarse meal.
4. Before beating the eggs, remove 2 tablespoons of the whites. Reserve.
5. Beat the eggs, and add, along with the cream, to the butter mixture.
6. Knead on a lightly floured board until the dough sticks together.
7. Divide dough in half.
8. Roll each half into a circle 6 inches in diameter, and 1-inch thick.
9. Cut the circles into quarters. You will have 8 triangles.
10. Brush the tops with the reserved egg whites and sprinkle with remaining 2 teaspoons sugar.
11. Place on greased cookie sheets and bake for 15 minutes. Serve immediately with sweet butter and jam.

YIELD: 8 scones
PREPARATION TIME: 15 minutes
BAKING TIME: 15 minutes

# ALMOND TEA BREAD

Although this is a very understated (and very good) quick bread, it will forever remind me of mid-morning play groups—those comforting get-togethers for moms and tots. We'd drink tea, and I often served this bread. It's a delicious bread that can be made quickly and served warm to guests of any age.

| | |
|---|---|
| ½ | cup butter (1 stick), at room temperature |
| ¾–1 | cup granulated sugar |
| 1 | egg |
| 2 | cups flour |
| ¼ | teaspoon baking powder |
| ¼ | teaspoon baking soda |
| ¼ | teaspoon salt |
| ½ | cup milk |
| ¼ | teaspoon almond extract |
| ¼ | teaspoon vanilla extract |
| ½ | cup sliced almonds, toasted |

1. Preheat oven to 325 degrees.
2. Cream the butter. Gradually blend in the sugar.
3. Mix in the egg until blended.
4. Sift together dry ingredients.
5. Add the dry ingredients alternating with the milk, starting and ending with the dry ingredients.
6. Stir until well blended.
7. Toast the almonds in a 325 degree oven for 5 minutes. Add along with the extracts to the mixture.
8. Pour into a greased loaf pan.
9. Bake for 1 hour or until a cake tester comes out clean.
10. Cool in pan for 5 minutes. Turn onto a wire rack to continue cooling.

YIELD: 1 loaf
PREPARATION TIME: under 30 minutes
BAKING TIME: 1 hour

# WHOLE WHEAT BLUEBERRY MUFFINS

I love sweets for breakfast: pastries, coffee cakes, and muffins. This is my favorite compromise—satisfyingly delicious and more wholesome than most.

| | |
|---|---|
| ¼ | cup butter |
| ½ | cup granulated sugar |
| 1 | egg, beaten |
| ¾ | cup milk |
| ¼ | teaspoon vanilla extract |
| ½ | cup whole wheat flour |
| ¼ | cup bran |
| 1 | cup unbleached white flour |
| 2½ | teaspoons baking powder |
| ½ | teaspoon salt |
| 1 | cup blueberries |

1. Heat oven to 425 degrees.
2. Cream butter and sugar. Add beaten egg and stir to combine.
3. Add milk and vanilla. Stir.
4. Combine flours and bran in a separate bowl. Reserve 1 tablespoon.
5. Add remaining dry ingredients and stir.
6. Combine dry mixture with creamed butter. Stir to moisten but do not over mix.
7. Coat berries with reserved 1 tablespoon flour.
8. Fold berries into batter.
9. Bake in 12 greased muffin tins for 20 minutes.

**YIELD:** 12 muffins
**PREPARATION TIME:** 15 minutes
**BAKING TIME:** 20 minutes

# CATHERINE'S OATMEAL AND MOLASSES BREAD

Inscribed inside my engagement ring is: 19 November 1893 CLF from APR. The ring belonged to my husband's great grandmother, Catherine Lucy Farr Robinson and this is her bread. It is everyone's favorite.

Besides its wonderful texture and flavor, this bread has an extra bonus: start it the night before (there is no kneading) and it rises overnight. Early risers can stir it down and pop it in the oven, and the rest of the household will awaken to the heavenly aroma and taste of warm bread. A very easy, very delicious recipe.

| | |
|---|---|
| 1 | cup oatmeal |
| 2 | cups boiling water |
| 1 | yeast cake |
| 3 | tablespoons warm water |
| ½ | cup black molasses |
| 1 | tablespoon salt |
| 4 | cups unbleached white flour |

Make this sponge the night before.

1. Soak the oatmeal for ½ hour in the water.
2. Dissolve yeast in the warm water. Add to oatmeal.
3. Stir in molasses and salt.
4. Slowly sift in flour.
5. Mix well with a wooden spoon.
6. Put in a bowl to rise overnight. Cover with a clean tea towel.

In the morning:

1. Preheat oven to 350 degrees.
2. Stir dough down and divide into two buttered loaf pans.
3. Let rise for about 1 hour.
4. Bake for 1 hour.

YIELD: 2 loaves
PREPARATION TIME: Less than ½ hour plus rising times
BAKING TIME: 1 hour

**VARIATION:** Substitute 1 cup whole wheat flour for 1 cup white flour.

# VERMONT UPSIDE-DOWN CAKE

Apples and maple syrup, of course! Turn this cake out of its pan and a flowery pattern of apples appears. Lovely for an outdoor autumn breakfast, as this cake isn't too sweet.

*Topping*

| | |
|---|---|
| 3 | tablespoons butter |
| ½ | cup pure maple syrup |
| 2 | tablespoons sliced almonds |
| 2 | apples (Macintosh), washed and cored, not peeled |

*Cake*

| | |
|---|---|
| 4 | tablespoons butter |
| ⅓ | cup granulated sugar |
| ½ | teaspoon vanilla extract |
| 2 | eggs |
| 1½ | cups flour |
| ¼ | teaspoon salt |
| 2 | teaspoons baking powder |
| ½ | cup milk |
| | Whipped cream |

1. Preheat oven to 350 degrees.
2. In an 8- or 9-inch iron skillet (or 9-inch cake pan), melt 3 tablespoons butter. Pour in maple syrup and sprinkle on almonds.
3. Slice apples in half-inch rings. Then, cut all the rings in half except one.
4. Place the single whole apple ring in the center of the buttery pan. Arrange the remaining slices in a ring around the central one. Set aside.
5. To prepare the batter, cream the 4 tablespoons butter with the sugar until light and fluffy. Beat in the vanilla. Add the eggs, one at a time, beating well after each addition.
6. Sift together the flour, salt, and baking powder. Add this to the creamed mixture in 3 parts, alternating with the milk. Combine well.
7. Pour the batter over the apples and bake for 45 minutes.
8. Remove from oven and cool in the pan for 5 minutes on a rack.
9. While still warm, turn upside down on a serving dish.
10. Serve warm and pass whipped cream separately.

**PREPARATION TIME: 15 minutes**
**BAKING TIME: 45 minutes**

# FILLED BISCUITS

These flaky biscuits have pork and apples baked inside them. They are a simplified version of Cornish pasties, the hardy and nutritious little meat and vegetable pies made for lunches by Cornish wives for their husbands working in the mines. What a warm and loving gesture I imagine those filling lunches to be, as I whip yet another peanut butter and honey sandwich into a brown paper bag.

We eat these biscuits warm from the oven with butter, adding salad or soup for a light dinner. Although this is a tidy way to use small quantities of leftover pork roast (some of us get inspired not wasting even the tiniest bit), I have also made it using two uncooked pork chops. Cut chops into small pieces, sauté meat with garlic, salt and pepper, and then proceed with recipe.

| | |
|---|---|
| 2 | cups flour |
| 1 | teaspoon salt |
| 2½ | teaspoons baking powder |
| 4 | tablespoons butter |
| ⅓ | cup milk |
| ⅓ | cup water |
| ½ | cup cooked, well-seasoned pork |
| ½ | cup apple, diced |

1. Preheat oven to 425 degrees.
2. Combine dry ingredients.
3. Cut the butter into flour mixture using 2 knives, until the mixture resembles coarse cornmeal.
4. While lightly tossing the butter-flour mixture with a fork, add the liquids. Stir until the dough holds together.
5. Turn dough onto a lightly floured board. Knead about 10 times.
6. Roll dough thin to ¼ inch or a bit less, if possible.
7. Cut into 2-inch rounds with a floured glass.
8. Put half of the cut biscuits on a baking sheet.

9. Combine diced pork and apple. Place about 1 tablespoon on each biscuit.
10. Cover with the remaining biscuits. Press edges together to seal for baking.
11. Bake for 12–15 minutes until lightly browned. Serve warm with butter.

YIELD: 10 2-inch biscuits
PREPARATION TIME: 30 minutes
BAKING TIME: 15 minutes

**VARIATIONS:** Both the fillings and the size and shape of these can be changed.
Add chutney or raisins to this filling. Fill biscuits with partially cooked sausage or ham and cheese. Smaller shapes can be served as an hors d'oeuvre. Try larger 8-inch circles folded in half to make turnovers. To borrow the Cornish pasty idea, stuff with leftovers such as cooked meat, grated carrots, potatoes, turnips, salt and pepper and make these turnovers into full meals. Experiment with your own combinations including leftover gravy or cream.

# PUMPKIN BISCUITS

When the days get cooler, we naturally cook warming foods and bake more. Particularly in the autumn, as fall colors slowly overtake the green hillside, so too, do my tastes turn to golden harvest foods. Crisp red apples and cinnamon-apple pies, golden yellow cornbreads and Indian puddings, baked maple squash, and pumpkin pies find their way onto our table.

Pumpkin biscuits are a true seasonal specialty, bright pumpkin orange, light and enticing. Gentle kneading and minimal handling of the dough will insure a flaky and tender biscuit.

| | |
|---|---|
| 2 | cups flour |
| 1 | tablespoon baking powder |
| 1 | teaspoon salt |
| ½ | teaspoon granulated sugar |
| | Pinch ginger and allspice |
| 6 | tablespoons butter (or butter/shortening combination) |
| ½ | cup pumpkin puree (canned pumpkin may be used but *not* pie filling) |
| ½ | cup milk |

1. Preheat oven to 425 degrees.
2. Combine dry ingredients.
3. Cut in the shortening until the mixture is crumbly, about the size of small peas.
4. Alternately add the pumpkin and the milk, beginning and ending with the pumpkin. Stir after each addition. Do not over mix; the mixture will not be completely blended.
6. Turn the dough onto a lightly floured board. Knead gently until the mixture just holds together.
7. Pat gently into a circle about ½-inch thick.
8. Cut out biscuits with a floured glass.
9. Bake on a greased cookie sheet for 15–18 minutes.

YIELD: 10 biscuits
PREPARATION TIME: 10 minutes
BAKING TIME: 15–18 minutes

# THE LOOKOUT
# LEMON PANCAKE

Summer or winter, the Lookout Lemon Pancake heralds a glorious day to follow. Easily made yet still very impressive, it takes less than a half hour from its beginnings to the table. Serve and enjoy it with your family and friends.

| | |
|---|---|
| ½ | cup flour |
| 2 | eggs |
| ½ | cup milk |
| | Pinch nutmeg |
| ¼ | teaspoon grated zest of 1 lemon or dried lemon peel |
| ¼ | pound butter (1 stick) |
| 2 | tablespoons powdered sugar |
| | Juice of ½ lemon |
| | Maple syrup and lemon juice (optional) |

1. Heat oven to 425 degrees.
2. Mix flour, eggs, milk, nutmeg and lemon zest in a bowl. Do not over mix; batter should be lumpy.
3. Melt all the butter in a 10-inch cast-iron skillet on top of the stove.
4. Pour batter into skillet.
5. Bake 15–20 minutes, until puffy and golden brown.
6. Sprinkle with the powdered sugar, through a small sieve, and return to oven for 1 minute.
7. Immediately before serving, squeeze most of the juice of ½ lemon over the top of the pancake.
8. Combine the remaining lemon juice with warm maple syrup, and pass in pitcher.

**YIELD: 4 servings**
**PREPARATION AND BAKING TIME: 30 minutes**

**VARIATIONS:** Instead of lemon juice and maple syrup, vary the toppings by heaping freshly stewed strawberries and rhubarb or melted apricot preserves with brandy in the center of the pancake. Try hot buttery apple slices sprinkled with cinnamon and, perhaps, flamed with Calvados.

# SWEET CHEESE-FILLED COFFEE CAKE

A not-too-sweet golden yeast cake, perfect for brunch. Try filling the center of tube cakes with daisies and field flowers for outdoor summer breakfasts.

*Cake*

| | |
|---|---|
| ½ | cup lukewarm milk |
| 1 | package yeast |
| 1 | teaspoon granulated sugar |
| ½ | cup flour |
| ¼ | cup granulated sugar |
| ½ | cup butter (1 stick) |
| 2 | eggs |
| ½ | teaspoon salt |
| 1 | teaspoon grated lemon or orange rind |
| 1¾ | cups flour |

*Filling*

| | |
|---|---|
| 6 | ounces cream cheese, at room temperature |
| 6 | tablespoons granulated sugar |
| 1 | large egg |
| ¾ | teaspoon vanilla extract |
| ⅓ | cup apricot jam, optional |

1. Pour lukewarm milk into a bowl. Sprinkle yeast and 1 teaspoon sugar on top. Stir to dissolve.
2. Stir in the ½ cup flour. Cover with a dish towel and let rise in a warm place, about 30 minutes.
3. In a large bowl, cream the butter with the ¼ cup sugar, until soft and light. Beat in the eggs. Add salt and rind.
4. Add the yeast sponge to the creamed mixture.
5. Gradually add 1¾ cups flour. Stir well.
6. Cover bowl and allow to rise until doubled in bulk, about 1½ to 2 hours.
7. To prepare the filling, cream the cheese until light, gradually adding the sugar.
8. Add the egg, beating until smooth. Stir in vanilla.
9. When the dough has risen, remove it from the bowl to waxed paper, and pat it into an oblong shape about ⅓-inch thick.

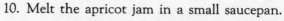

10. Melt the apricot jam in a small saucepan.

11. Spread some of it (sparingly) over the dough.

12. Gently spread cream cheese mixture over the dough.

13. Roll dough from a long side to encase filling, forming a long tube shape.

14. Pull gently to shape it into a greased 9-inch tube pan. Pinch closed any tears, and join ends together to form a ring.

15. Preheat oven to 350 degrees.

16. Cover the ring and allow to rise for an additional thirty minutes.

17. Bake for 30 minutes.

18. Allow to cool 10 minutes on a rack.

19. Turn out. Spread remaining apricot glaze over top of cake or ice with a powdered sugar and milk glaze.

**PREPARATION TIME: 30 minutes plus
  2½ hours rising time
BAKING TIME: 30 minutes**

# SARAH'S PUMPKIN BREAD

This is Sarah's yearly contribution to Wild Farm's Thanksgiving. No one would have it any other way.

Pumpkin bread is especially delicious spread with cream cheese. Be sure to put some aside for Pumpkim Bread Pudding (see page 126).

| | |
|---|---|
| ⅔ | cup butter |
| 2⅔ | cups granulated sugar |
| 4 | eggs |
| 1 | pound prepared pumpkin |
| ⅔ | cup water |
| 3⅓ | cups flour |
| ½ | teaspoon baking soda |
| 1½ | teaspoons salt |
| 1 | teaspoon cinnamon |
| 1 | teaspoon ground cloves |
| ⅔ | cup chopped walnuts |
| ⅔ | cup chopped dates |

1. Preheat oven to 350 degrees.
2. Cream butter and sugar until fluffy.
3. Beat in 4 eggs, pumpkin and water.
4. Sift together dry ingredients, and stir into pumpkin mixture.
5. Fold in nuts and dates.
6. Spoon batter into 2 loaf pans. Bake for 1 hour.

YIELD: 2 loaves
PREPARATION TIME: 25 minutes
BAKING TIME: 1 hour

# APRICOT BREAKFAST PASTRIES

Actually these are just wonderful anytime, for dessert or a mid-morning snack. They are very easy; prepare ahead and refrigerate or freeze them. Pop in the oven before serving. Apricot pastries are the very best way I know to use leftover trimmings from a Sour Cream Pie Crust.

½ recipe of Sour Cream Pastry (see page 151), or pastry leftovers

Apricot preserves, good quality

Chopped walnuts

1. Preheat oven to 350 degrees.
2. Prepare pastry (or use leftovers). Roll on a lightly floured board to a thickness of ⅛ inch.
3. With a pastry wheel or knife, cut into strips 1" x 3".
4. Spread a bit of apricot jam on each pastry strip and sprinkle with chopped walnuts.
5. Roll up. Place seam down on baking sheet. Bake until they are light brown and flaky, about 8–10 minutes.

**PREPARATION TIME: 5 minutes**
**BAKING TIME: 8 minutes**

# Country Suppers

# SUNDAY AFTERNOON

Autumn is the busiest time; the garden is harvested, wood stacked, the house readied for winter. The beautiful days invigorate us, transforming the outside chores to pleasing rituals.

When winter comes, we settle inside; afternoons linger, we read more and visit with friends. I love Sunday afternoons; dinner is simmering on the stove and we can relax with company. We play Dictionary, or Charades, or listen to plays on the radio. We feel warm by the fire and cozy in our togetherness.

Hot drinks are good ways to keep the chill away.

## SOUTH WINDS SPIRIT CREAM

| | |
|---|---|
| 1 | beaten egg |
| 1 | cup milk |
| 1 | cup heavy cream |
| ¼ | cup coffee brandy or liqueur |
| 2 | tablespoons bourbon |
| 2 | teaspoons granulated sugar |
| 1 | teaspoon instant coffee powder |

1. Combine all ingredients in a heavy-bottomed saucepan.
2. Cook and stir over low heat until thickened, about 7 or 8 minutes.
3. Serve in small mugs or demitasse cups.

# PIZZA RUSTICA

This is a double-crusted, deep dish pizza. Truly a country dish, it benefits from the creative use of any on-hand ingredients or a fanciful raid of your garden. Your imagination and options will give Pizza Rustica its character. You may just hit upon the ultimate combination. Served with a green salad, it is a hearty, fun, and satisfying meal.

| | |
|---|---|
| 1 | **9-inch double pastry crust, your own (see page 150) or frozen** |
| 1 | **tablespoon butter, softened to room temperature** |
| 3 | **eggs** |
| 1 | **cup ricotta cheese** |
| ½ | **pound mozzarella cheese, cut in small cubes** |
| 1 | **cup plum tomatoes, drained, chopped, and drained again** |
| ¼ | **cup freshly grated Parmesan cheese** |
| 2–3 | **cups filling options: ham pieces, sausage, mushrooms, proscuitto, black or green olives, mushrooms, pimento, broccoli, cheeses, spinach, red or green peppers, fresh herbs, etc.** |

1. Preheat oven to 375 degrees.
2. Prepare pastry and fit into bottom of a 9-inch deep dish. Spread with 1 tablespoon butter.
3. Beat eggs and ricotta until creamy. Stir in remaining ingredients, including filling options.
4. Spoon into pastry. Cover with top crust. Trim and crimp edges.
5. Bake 45 minutes.

YIELD: 4–6 servings
PREPARATION TIME: Under 30 minutes, excluding crust
BAKING TIME: 45 minutes

# A NEW ENGLAND CASSOULET

Cassoulet is the celebrated dish from southwestern France. Each region produces its own variation, emphasizing local specialties. While ingredients and complexity can vary, most cassoulets are based on white beans and include some of the following: *confite d'oie* (preserved goose) or duck, mutton, pork, ham, sausage, bacon. The preserved goose gives it authenticity, but a very decent dish can be made without it. The following is "our regional version" . . . an elegant country supper. Serve cassoulet in the dish it is prepared in; an earthenware dish is traditional. It can be prepared ahead (leave bread topping off) and be reheated.

| | |
|---|---|
| 1½–2 | **pounds dried white beans, soaked overnight, in cold water to cover** |
| 2 | **onions, chopped** |
| ½ | **teaspoon salt** |
| ¼ | **teaspoon thyme** |
| 1 | **bay leaf** |
| 1 | **tablespoon chopped parsley** |
| 1 | **pound pork link sausage** |
| ½ | **pound lean salt pork** |
| 4 | **tablespoons fat (lard, pork trimmings, butter)** |
| 2 | **pounds boned shoulder or leg of lamb, cut in 1-inch cubes** |
| 2 | **cloves garlic, minced** |
| ½ | **teaspoon salt** |
| 2 | **tablespoons tomato paste** |

1. Drain beans after soaking overnight. Put in a large saucepan and cover with cold water.
2. Add onions, salt, thyme, bay leaf, parsley, sausage and salt pork.
3. Bring to a boil and simmer for 30 minutes. Remove sausage and continue to simmer for 1 hour longer.
4. Meanwhile, in a large skillet, melt butter or fat. Add lamb, the minced garlic, and salt. Cook until lamb browns lightly.
5. Add some liquid from the bean pot to cover the lamb. Mix in tomato paste and pepper. Simmer for about 1 hour. Stir and add additional liquid to the beans as needed.
6. Preheat oven to 300 degrees.
7. Drain beans. Reserve liquid.
8. Remove salt pork and cut in small ½-inch cubes.
9. Slice sausage in ½-inch pieces.
10. Combine sausage, salt pork and lamb and set aside.
11. Rub a large earthenware casserole with the split clove of garlic.

| | Freshly ground pepper |
|---|---|
| 1 | clove garlic, split |
| 2 | tablespoons chopped parsley |
| 1 | cup fresh bread crumbs |
| 2–3 | tablespoons butter |

12. Put a third of the beans in the dish. Next add half the meat, another third of beans, the remaining meat, then the remaining beans.

13. Pour in juices from the lamb skillet and enough bean liquid to cover. Bake, covered, for 1 hour.

14. Uncover, add a bit more bean liquid, if needed to almost cover and sprinkle with bread crumbs and parsley. Dot with 2–3 tablespoons of butter.

15. Return to oven, uncovered, for an additional 30 minutes or so. Topping should be brown and crusty. Serve from the casserole.

**YIELD: 8–10 servings**
**COOKING TIME: 4½ hours**

**VARIATIONS:** This is a country dish; do not be afraid to try your own versions using meats you have available—leftover poultry, pork chops, sausage patties, or ham hocks, layered among the beans. White wine or vermouth can be used for part of the lamb braising liquid in step five.

# CHICKEN PLAZA PIE

I just love chicken pies, one of the all-time comforting foods for me. Chicken Plaza Pie seems like such a relaxed dish to prepare, maybe because like chicken soup, it is hard to rush it, or maybe because it only occurs to me to make it when I have the time to linger in the kitchen.

My version of chicken pie mixes the traditional tastes of pastry, gravy and chicken with less traditional vegetables: mushrooms, pearl onions and broccoli. You, of course, can vary the vegetables: artichoke hearts and leeks lend it new elegance; peas, carrots, celery, onions, turnips, pimento make it downright homey. Lots of delicious choices.

| | |
|---|---|
| ½ | cup pearl onions |
| 6 | tablespoons butter |
| 12 | mushrooms, quartered |
| 6 | tablespoons flour |
| 1½ | cups chicken broth |
| 1 | cup cream |
| 2 | tablespoons Cognac or sherry |
| 1½ | cups cooked chicken, cut in fork-sized pieces |
| ¾–1 | cup cooked broccoli or canned artichoke hearts, cut in small pieces |
| 1 | sheet frozen puff pastry, or your own pastry (see page 150) |

1. First prepare the onions: Cut a shallow cross into the root end of each onion. Put onions in boiling water and simmer for 5 minutes. Remove with a slotted spoon and dip in cold water. Peel skins and set onions aside.

2. Melt butter in a skillet. Toss in mushrooms and sauté for a few minutes. Whisk in flour and stir 3 minutes.

3. Pour in broth and cream. Bring to a boil, stirring occasionally. Add Cognac or sherry; simmer until slightly thickened.

4. Preheat oven to 375 degrees.

5. Stir chicken, broccoli, and onions into cream sauce.

6. Pour chicken filling into a deep oven dish or casserole.

7. Cut pastry the shape of casserole top with a 1-inch overhang.

8. Gently place pastry over the casserole with pastry overhanging casserole edges. Do not trim.

9. Bake for 30 minutes.

YIELD: 6 servings
PREPARATION TIME: 40 minutes
BAKING TIME: 30 minutes

# HAM IN TARRAGON CREAM SAUCE

Thick slices of sautéed ham in a rich tarragon-flavored cream sauce. Prepare ahead up to the addition of the cream. Just prior to serving, add the cream, simmer, and reheat ham in sauce. Serve with crisp, sautéed, walnut-sized potato rounds.

| | |
|---|---|
| 2 | pounds cooked ham, sliced ⅓-inch thick |
| 2 | tablespoons butter |
| 1 | tablespoon oil |
| 2 | shallots, very finely chopped |
| ½ | teaspoon dried tarragon or 1½ teaspoons fresh |
| 1 | tablespoon flour |
| ½ | cup Madeira or vermouth |
| 1 | tablespoon Cognac (optional) |
| 1 | tablespoon tarragon wine vinegar or white wine vinegar |
| 1 | teaspoon tomato paste |
| ½ | teaspoon Dijon-style mustard |
| ½ | cup heavy cream |

1. Dry ham slices with a paper towel. Trim off excess fat. Cut ham slices in 2 or 3 large pieces if meat is too large for skillet.

2. Add a piece of the trimmed fat to 1 tablespoon butter and oil in large skillet. When fat is hot, lightly brown ham on both sides. Remove to a warm platter.

3. Drain most of the fat from the pan. Add the remaining 1 tablespoon butter, shallots and tarragon. Cook over low heat for 1 minute.

4. Add flour; stir with a wire whisk for 2 minutes more.

5. Add Madeira and Cognac. Bring to a boil, and then simmer for 5 minutes.

6. Blend vinegar, tomato paste and mustard into the sauce. Continue to simmer, partially covered for 10 minutes more.

7. Add the cream to the skillet. Return to a simmer and allow to reduce slightly.

8. Return ham and any juices to the skillet. Heat through.

9. Spoon sauce over ham. Arrange ham on a serving platter and garnish with sprigs of tarragon or other greens.

YIELD: 4 servings
COOKING TIME: 30 minutes

# ROAST LOIN OF PORK ON A BED OF RED CABBAGE

On the chilliest nights, this classic combination of pork and cabbage is a welcome treat. In this version, the cabbage is further enriched by the pork drippings, making it extra flavorful and hearty. Dark bread, and hard cider or beer round the meal out.

### Cabbage

| | |
|---|---|
| 4 | tablespoons butter |
| 1 | small red cabbage, quartered, cored and sliced |
| 2 | tablespoons lemon juice (or red wine) |
| 1 | large apple (or 2 small), quartered, cored and sliced |
| 1/8 | teaspoon ground cloves |
| 1 | tablespoon granulated sugar |

### Pork

| | |
|---|---|
| 3–4 | pound pork loin, boned and tied |
| 1 | teaspoon salt |
| 1/2 | teaspoon freshly ground pepper |
| 1/2 | teaspoon thyme |
| 1 | clove garlic, mashed |

1. If using the optional dry marinade, rub a paste of salt, pepper, thyme, and garlic over the roast, and let it sit for 2 hours or longer.

2. To prepare cabbage, put 2 inches of water in a pot. Add butter and bring to a boil.

3. Add sliced cabbage, lemon juice, apples, cloves, and sugar.

4. Stir and cook gently, covered, for 20 minutes.

5. Mound the cabbage in a roasting pan.

6. Preheat oven to 325 degrees.

7. If meat has been marinating, rub off the dry marinade. Otherwise, rub a paste of salt and garlic over the roast.

8. Brown meat quickly, on all sides, in a skillet on top of the stove.

9. Place browned roast on top of the red cabbage.

10. Put in oven for 25–30 minutes per pound, or until meat thermometer reads 165–170 degrees.

11. Occasionally stir the cabbage, and baste the roast with wine or water. Keep the cabbage moist, adding liquid if necessary.

12. Remove the roast from oven and let sit 10–15 minutes before carving.

13. Place roast on a heated serving platter. Carve a few slices, and leave remaining roast whole to be sliced as needed at the table. Surround roast with red cabbage.

**YIELD:** 10–12 servings
**MARINATION TIME:** 2 hours
**PREPARATION TIME:** 30 minutes
**ROASTING TIME:** 25–30 minutes per pound

**VARIATIONS:** Baste meat with apple cider, juice or brandy. Heat 2 tablespoons brandy in a small pan, ignite and pour over the roast just before putting it in the oven.

# A BEEF STEW PROVENCAL

Definitely for lovers of olives, this stew marries the wonderful flavors of Provence. It is an excellent informal party dish because it can be cooked a day in advance. Reheating it will only improve the flavor. Serve the stew from the casserole it was cooked in, with small whole boiled potatoes and buttered *petits pois*.

| | |
|---|---|
| 1/3 | cup parsley |
| 2 | cloves garlic |
| | Freshly ground black pepper |
| 1 | tablespoon olive oil |
| 2 | slices bacon |
| 2 | pounds beef stew meat, cut in 1½-inch cubes |
| 2 | tablespoons flour |
| 2 | tablespoons brandy |
| 1½ | cups white wine (use red wine for a heartier flavor) |
| ½ | cup water |
| 2 | teaspoons tomato paste |
| ¼ | teaspoon thyme |
| 20 | pitted olives, a combination of black and green |
| | Salt and pepper |

1. Mince together parsley, garlic and black pepper.
2. Cut uncooked bacon into 2-inch pieces. Cook with olive oil in a large casserole over a gentle heat until bacon begins to render its fat and browns. Remove bacon with slotted spoon.
3. Coat stew beef in the parsley mixture.
4. Raise heat and brown the meat in the bacon fat on all sides.
5. Add the flour, and stir gently for 2 minutes.
6. Pour in the brandy, wine, and water. Stir in the tomato paste, and thyme.
7. Cover and simmer for 1½ hours.
8. Uncover. Add the olives for an additional ½ hour of cooking.
9. Season to taste with salt and pepper.

YIELD: 6 servings
PREPARATION TIME: 30 minutes
COOKING TIME: 2 hours

**VARIATIONS:** Substitute or add mushrooms and pearl onions for the olives. Add after 1 hour of cooking. Add the flour to the parsley mixture before dredging the meat. After browning the meat, heat the brandy, ignite and pour over the braised meat.

# BAKED RED ONION AND GARLIC SOUP AU GRATIN

| | |
|---|---|
| 4 | medium-sized red onions, thinly sliced |
| 3 | cloves garlic, chopped (or less if you prefer a milder garlic taste) |
| 3 | tablespoons butter |
| 2 | tablespoons oil |
| ½ | teaspoon salt |
| 1 | teaspoon granulated sugar |
| 3 | tablespoons flour |
| 9 | cups beef stock or broth (a good canned broth will do) |
| ¾ | cup dry vermouth or white wine |
| 3 | tablespoons Cognac |
| | Slices of French bread |
| 1½ | cups grated cheeses, Swiss or cheddar |
| ⅓ | cup grated hard cheese, Parmesan or Romano |
| | Freshly ground pepper |
| 2 | tablespoons butter |

1. In a Dutch oven, heat onions and garlic together in the butter and oil. Cover and cook over low heat 15 minutes, until onions are translucent.
2. Stir in the salt and sugar; raise heat to medium.
3. Stir frequently until onions are a deep brown. This will take 30–35 minutes. Keep stirring to keep from burning.
4. Sprinkle flour over onions, stirring for a few minutes.
5. Add broth and vermouth; bring to a boil. Simmer over low heat for half an hour.
6. Stir in Cognac.
7. Heat slices of French bread in a low oven for 5 minutes.
8. Ladle soup over bread. Bread will float to the top.
9. Top bread with cheeses. Grind on pepper and dot with butter.
10. Bake in 400 degree oven, for about ½ hour until soup is bubbly and top is brown.
11. Serve immediately.

YIELD: 4–6 servings
COOKING TIME: 1½ hours
BAKING TIME: 30 minutes

# SWEET AND SOUR CABBAGE SOUP

A sweet and sour soup very much like Grandma's (some things are better left unaltered). Like many hearty soups, this benefits from a slow simmer and being made at least a day in advance, although it isn't absolutely necessary. There is enough meat in the soup to serve it along with Catherine's Oatmeal Bread (see page 16) or Whole Wheat Blueberry Muffins (see page 15) for a very satisfying lunch.

| | |
|---|---|
| 1½ | pounds fresh brisket, flank or chuck steak, trimmed of fat and cut into thin strips |
| 2 | tablespoons butter |
| 1 | head cabbage, cut into 1-inch pieces or coarsely shredded |
| 1 | large onion, chopped |
| 1 | (8-ounce) can of tomato sauce |
| ½ | cup tomatoes, drained and chopped |
| 3 | tablespoons brown sugar |
| 2 | tablespoons lemon juice |
| 2 | teaspoons paprika |
| 1 | teaspoon salt |
| 2 | cups coarsely grated carrots |
| 7 | cups water |
| ½ | teaspoon sour salt (also known as citric acid), optional |

1. Melt butter over high heat in a 5-quart soup pot.
2. Add meat, cabbage, onion and cook for 15 minutes. Stir often until the cabbage is tender.
3. Add tomato sauce, tomatoes, brown sugar, lemon juice, paprika, salt, and water.
4. Bring to a boil; then cover and simmer for 1 hour.
5. Add the carrots; simmer for an additional 30 minutes.
6. Stir in the optional sour salt. Add additional salt and pepper to taste.

YIELD: 8 servings
PREPARATION TIME: 25 minutes
COOKING TIME: 1 hour 45 minutes

# POTATOES AU GRATIN WITH LEEKS AND HAM

A satisfying winter supper, with Pears in Creme Carmel (see page 129) for dessert.

| | |
|---|---|
| 4 | medium to large potatoes, peeled and sliced ¼-inch thick |
| 2 | cups milk |
| | Pinch nutmeg, salt and pepper |
| 2 | tablespoons butter |
| 2 | leeks, white part only, split and rinsed |
| 1 | clove garlic, minced |
| 8 | ounces ham slice, ¼-inch thick, cut in 1-inch pieces |
| 1½ | cups grated Swiss cheese |
| 2 | tablespoons cream |
| 2 | tablespoons butter |
| 2 | tablespoons grated Parmesan cheese |

1. Bring milk, salt, pepper and nutmeg to a simmer. Add potatoes and cook 15 minutes or until tender.

2. Melt butter in a skillet. Add leeks and garlic; stir over medium-low heat to soften leeks. Add ham, raise heat and stir for 2 minutes more.

3. Heat oven to 400 degrees.

4. Lightly butter an oval ceramic or enamel baking dish. Spread a thin layer of ham and leeks, then half the potatoes. Sprinkle on more pepper and half of the grated Swiss cheese. Layer the rest of the ham, then the rest of the potatoes. Sprinkle more pepper and the remaining Swiss cheese.

5. Pour the cream over all. Dot with the butter and add the grated Parmesan cheese.

6. Bake for 30 minutes until browned and bubbly.

**YIELD: 4 servings**
**PREPARATION TIME: 20 minutes**
**BAKING TIME: 30 minutes**

# COUNTRY PORK SUPPER

A good dish anytime of year. Both the cabbage and pork chops can be made ahead of time; the cabbage can set in the refrigerator for two days, but the pork should be made early on the day it is to be served. Assemble all ingredients just before baking.

The cabbage is excellent, too, when served surrounding a pork roast. Simply deglaze pan with the cider and brandy, sprinkle with the bread crumbs and cheese, and bake 20 minutes.

*Cabbage*

| | |
|---|---|
| 1 | large cabbage, about 10 cups, coarsely chopped |
| 2 | tablespoons butter |
| 2 | cloves garlic, minced |
| 1 | medium onion, coarsely chopped |
| 2 | apples, cored and cut in eighths |
| | Salt and pepper |

*Pork Chops*

| | |
|---|---|
| 6 | loin pork chops, ½- to ¾-inch thick |
| 3 | tablespoons oil and butter combination |
| ½ | cup apple cider or juice |
| 2 | tablespoons brandy or Calvados (optional) |

1. Bring 2 inches of water to a boil in a large pot. Cook cabbage about 3 minutes. Drain.

2. In a large skillet, melt butter. Sauté onion and garlic over low heat, stirring until translucent, not brown. Add apples and cabbage, salt and pepper. Stir for another 3 minutes. Set aside in a bowl.

3. Pat pork chops dry with a paper towel. Season with salt and pepper.

4. In the same skillet used for the apple-cabbage mixture, heat the oil and butter. When hot, add chops and brown for a few minutes on each side. Remove and set aside.

5. Add cider and brandy to deglaze pan. Boil rapidly and reduce liquid by half.

6. Pour this liquid over the cabbage mixture. Preheat oven to 350 degrees.

*Assembly*

| | |
|---|---|
| ½ | **cup cream, scalded (optional)** |
| 1 | **bay leaf** |
| 2 | **tablespoons bread crumbs** |
| 2 | **tablespoons freshly grated Parmesan cheese** |

7. Use a covered heavy oven dish, large enough to hold a single layer of 3 chops. Spread ⅓ of the cabbage in the bottom of the dish; then layer 3 chops, then a second layer of cabbage, the second layer of chops. Finish with a layer of cabbage.

8. Pour optional scalded cream over all. Lay bay leaf on top and sprinkle on bread crumbs and cheese.

9. Bake, covered, for 30 minutes. Remove cover and bake an additional 5 to 10 minutes.

**YIELD:** 4–6 servings
**PREPARATION TIME:** 45 minutes
**BAKING TIME:** 40 minutes

# LAMB AND ZUCCHINI STEW WITH LEMON SAUCE

Stew needn't be heavy or wintery as Lamb and Zucchini Stew proves —light, fresh, invigorating flavors appropriate to warmer weather too.
    Cook the lamb and vegetables a day ahead if you like, but make the lemon sauce right before serving. Serve with a simple parsley rice, warmed French bread with sweet butter, and a good red Bourdeaux.

| | |
|---|---|
| ¼ | cup olive oil |
| 2 | pounds boneless shoulder of lamb, cut in 1-inch cubes |
| 1 | large onion, chopped |
| 2 | cloves garlic, minced |
| | Salt and pepper |
| 2 | cups water |
| 2 | medium zucchini, or 3 small |

*Sauce*

| | |
|---|---|
| 3 | eggs |
| | Juice of 2 lemons |
| 1¾ | cups pan drippings from cooked lamb (approximate) |
| | Salt and pepper, to taste |
| | Chopped parsley |

1. Heat the oil in a stew pot. Brown the lamb with onion and garlic. Season with salt and pepper.

2. Add water and simmer for 1½ hours.

3. Cut zucchini in ½-inch thick slices. Add to the lamb. Simmer for 10 minutes more, or until meat is tender.

4. Remove meat and zucchini with a slotted spoon to a dish, reserving cooking liquid, and keep warm while you prepare the sauce.

5. Beat the three eggs until foamy. Slowly add lemon juice, while you continue beating.

6. Gradually add the pan drippings from the cooked lamb, beating until slightly thickened.

7. Pour the sauce over the lamb and zucchini. Garnish with parsley. Serve hot.

YIELD: 6 servings
PREPARATION TIME: 15 minutes
COOKING TIME: 1½ hours

**VARIATIONS:** Change or mix vegetables: brocolli, green beans, cauliflower would all be good with the lemony sauce.

# POHOQUALINE BUTTERMILK PANCAKES

At Wild Farm, the sap is boiled down early every spring and the resulting maple syrup is regarded as a greatly appreciated reward and treat. Only the very best pancakes are worthy, and these more than qualify.

They originate from the Pohoqualine Fishing Club, a lodge in the Pocono Mountains where my husband's grandparents would go to fish. Grandma Ingersoll was so taken by these pancakes that she requested the recipe, as I eventually did from her.

| | |
|---|---|
| 2 | eggs, separated |
| ½ | teaspoon salt |
| 2 | cups buttermilk |
| 1 | cup flour |
| 1 | tablespoon oil |
| 1 | teaspoon baking soda |
| 1 | tablespoon warm water |

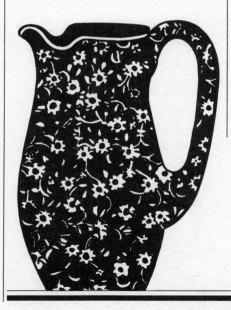

1. Combine egg yolks, salt, buttermilk, flour and oil. Mix well.

2. Dissolve baking soda in the warm water and add to the flour mixture.

3. Beat egg whites until stiff and fold into batter.

4. Grease a large skillet or griddle with shortening. Heat until a drop of water will sizzle on it.

5. Ladle batter into skillet. Pancakes should be small, about 3 inches in diameter.

6. When bubbles form around the edges, flip pancakes and cook 1–2 minutes more.

7. Serve with warm maple syrup, swirled with butter.

YIELD: 4–5 servings
PREPARATION TIME: 10 minutes

# TORTELLINI IN A SAUSAGE CREAM SAUCE

Easily made at the last minute, tortellini makes a quick and delicious meal. Most often served at dinnertime, I think it makes a welcome and special lunch for friends.

| | |
|---|---|
| 1 | 8-ounce package of tortellini |
| ½ | pound good quality lean bulk sausage |
| | Olive oil, as needed |
| 1 | clove garlic, minced |
| ½ | teaspoon rosemary (optional) |
| | Freshly ground pepper |
| 1 | cup light cream |
| ⅓ | cup freshly grated Parmesan cheese (or part cheddar) |

1. Cook pasta according to package directions.
2. While pasta is cooking, brown sausage in a skillet. Depending on the fat in the sausage, add oil if needed to keep sausage from sticking, or drain, if fat is excessive.
3. Stir in garlic, rosemary and pepper. Cook a few minutes more.
4. Add cream. When mixture begins to bubble, add the cheese.
5. Put tortellini on a warm platter. Spoon sausage sauce over, toss, and serve immediately. Garnish with parsley.

YIELD: 4–6 servings
PREPARATION TIME: 15 minutes

VARIATIONS: Finely chop a small onion and add to browning sausage. Add a scant tablespoon of flour to the sausage before adding the cream, for a thicker sauce.

# HOT STUFFED ITALIAN BREAD

Wrap this right from the broiler in foil and several layers of newspaper. Take it on a cool-weather picnic. At home, serve it as either an open-faced sandwich or, close and slice in 4-inch pieces. Children love the opportunity to build their own sandwiches—an ideal snack for after sledding. The ingredients are flexible and given here for one loaf of bread. Adjust accordingly.

| | |
|---|---|
| 2 | tablespoons olive oil |
| 2 | cloves garlic, finely chopped |
| 1 | cup drained tomatoes |
| ¼ | cup red or white wine |
| | Salt and pepper |
| | Pinch basil |
| 1 | baguette or similar long loaf of French or Italian bread |
| 6–8 | slices Genoa salami |
| 6–8 | slices provolone cheese |
| | Red onions |
| | Red and green peppers, optional to taste |
| | Black olives, optional to taste |
| | Freshly grated Parmesan cheese |

1. Heat olive oil and garlic together. Do not let garlic brown. Add tomatoes and simmer gently for 5 minutes. Add wine, bring to a boil, and reduce sauce by half. Add seasonings.

2. Split loaf of bread lengthwise and brush with olive oil. Spread 2–3 tablespoons of sauce over each half of bread.

3. Depending on width of bread, slice salami and cheese in half, if necessary. Alternate layers of meat and cheese.

4. Sprinkle with chopped onions, peppers and olives. Drizzle with additional olive oil and sprinkle with cheese.

5. Place 5–6 inches under broiler and heat for 4 minutes. Watch to keep from burning.

**YIELD: 2–4 servings**
**PREPARATION TIME: 15 minutes**

# LEONA'S TOURTIERE

This meat pie is traditional French Canadian fare for Christmas Eve, but it makes a hearty country supper on any cold winter's night, and is especially satisfying in late autumn when the bite of the brisk evening air still takes you by surprise.

The secret to a wonderful meat pie is the long slow simmer. Tourtiere is often served with scalloped potatoes; we like it with the Golden Potato Puree (see page 101). Pass a heaping bowl of sweet tongue pickles or your family's favorite bread and butter pickle slices.

**Pastry for double crust 8- or 9-inch pie (see page 150)**

| | |
|---|---|
| 1½ | pounds ground pork |
| 1 | large potato, cooked and mashed |
| 1 | onion, chopped fine |
| | Salt and pepper |
| ½ | teaspoon cinnamon |
| ¼ | teaspoon ground cloves |
| ½ | cup water |

1. Peel and boil 1 large potato. Mash.

2. Combine all ingredients in large skillet and simmer until thickened, about 1 hour. Be sure filling stays moist. Add more water if necessary.

3. While filling simmers, prepare pastry for crusts.

4. Preheat oven to 400 degrees.

5. Roll out bottom crust, ladle in filling and cover with top crust. Put aluminum foil around edges of pie to prevent burning during baking.

6. Bake for 50 minutes until golden.

7. Serve immediately, or cool on wire rack.

8. Meat pies can be prepared ahead and frozen for later use.

**YIELD: 6 servings**
**COOKING TIME: 1 hour**
**BAKING TIME: 50 minutes**

# SAUSAGE AND CHEESE SOUFFLÉ

Excellent for any meal. Readied ahead of time (or the night before if served at brunch), this soufflé allows you extra time for the little details that make entertaining fun: violets sitting pretty in grapefruit centers, heart-molded raspberry-flavored cream cheese, cloth napkins tied with ribbons and flowers at each setting.

| | |
|---|---|
| 6 | slices stale bread, white or a light whole wheat |
| 2 | tablespoons butter |
| 1 | pound good quality bulk sausage |
| ¼ | pound cheddar cheese, grated |
| 2 | eggs, well beaten |
| 1½ | teaspoons Dijon-style mustard |
| 2 | cups milk |

1. Remove crusts and lightly butter the bread.
2. Cook sausage until brown. Drain if excessive fat.
3. In a buttered soufflé dish, alternate layers of bread, sausage and cheese.
4. Mix together the eggs, mustard and milk. Pour over the layered bread, and let stand at least 4 hours or overnight. Return to room temperature prior to baking.
5. Preheat oven to 375 degrees. Bake 45 minutes and serve immediately.

YIELD: 4–6 servings
PREPARATION TIME: 30 minutes
REFRIGERATION TIME: 4 hours or overnight
BAKING TIME: 45 minutes

# BABOOTIE

A favorite pot luck offering that never grows tired. I serve it often and it still is a pleasant surprise of unusual ingredients. This is easily made ahead and can be refrigerated for a day or two or frozen.

| | |
|---|---|
| 2 | pounds ground lamb or beef |
| 2 | onions, grated |
| 2 | cloves garlic, minced |
| 16 | ounces tomatoes |
| 1½ | tablespoons granulated sugar |
| 2 | tablespoons curry powder |
| 2 | tablespoons cider vinegar |
| | Pinch salt |
| 2 | firm bananas |
| 1 | apple, peeled and chopped |
| 1 | tablespoon apricot jam |

1. Brown meat in a large skillet; drain off the fat.
2. Add the remaining ingredients, breaking up bananas with a wooden spoon.
3. Cover and simmer gently for 30 minutes.
4. Serve piping hot with rice or buttered noodles. Pass bowls of peanuts, flaked coconut, raisins and your favorite chutney.

YIELD: 8 servings
PREPARATON TIME: Under 30 minutes
COOKING TIME: 30 minutes

# GREEN BEANS, POTATOES AND CORNMEAL DUMPLINGS

This is good use for those big beans that were left on the vine too long. A frugal farm dish that tastes good wherever and however you live.

| | |
|---|---|
| 2 | pounds green beans |
| ¼ | pound chunk salt pork or bacon |
| ½ | teaspoon salt |
| 4 | medium potatoes |

*Dumplings*

| | |
|---|---|
| 1 | cup flour |
| 1 | teaspoon salt |
| 2 | teaspoons baking powder |
| 1 | cup cornmeal |
| 1 | egg, beaten |
| ¾ | cup milk |

1. Place beans, salt pork, and salt in a large pot. Add water almost to cover.

2. Cover pot and bring to a boil. Uncover and slowly simmer for 20 minutes.

3. Wash, halve, and if desired, peel the potatoes. Add to simmering liquid and cook 30 minutes more.

4. While simmering, prepare dumplings. Combine dry ingredients. In a separate bowl, mix the egg and milk together. Combine egg mixture with dry ingredients. Do not over mix.

5. Drop by rounded teaspoonful on top of the boiling greens and potatoes. Cover pot and cook for 15 minutes.

6. Serve beans, potatoes and dumplings with chopped bacon or salt pork and pot juices if desired.

**YIELD: 4 servings**
**PREPARATION TIME: 15 minutes**
**COOKING TIME: 65 minutes**

# BARBECUED CHUTNEY CHICKEN

Marinate the chicken well in advance; then, barbecue or broil it. Try serving it with rice salad, fried green tomatoes, and warm corn bread. Pass bowls of homemade chutney.

| | |
|---|---|
| 6 | boneless chicken breasts, skinned |
| ½ | cup chutney |
| ½ | cup lime juice |
| 1–2 | tablespoons yogurt |
| ¼ | teaspoon dry mustard |
| ½ | teaspoon curry powder |
| | Slices of avocado |

1. Cut breasts in half to make 12 small pieces.
2. Combine remaining ingredients to make a marinade.
3. Arrange chicken pieces in a shallow dish and cover with marinade.
4. Turn chicken over several times to coat with marinade.
5. Cover with plastic wrap and marinate at least 3 hours unrefrigerated—4 hours or longer in refrigerator.
6. Cook on a grill over grayish coals until done—about 4 minutes per side.
7. Garnish serving platter with avocado slices, sprinkled with lime juice. Pass bowls of chutney.

YIELD: 5–6 servings
PREPARATION TIME: 15 minutes
COOKING TIME: 10 minutes
MARINATE: 3 or more hours

# ORANGE RICE AND CHICKEN ALMANDINE

This recipe is a treasure of versatility. It is a simply prepared everyday dish but the flavors are interesting enough to be the basis of special company meals. Begin the meal with individual servings of spinach, barely cooked snowpeas, and red onions tossed in a light Soy Vinaigrette (see page 105). Serve the chicken along with broccoli, and herbed popovers with orange butter.

For an unusual and delicious picnic, bone the cooked chicken and toss with the rice, almonds and sauce. Chill.

*Rice*

| | |
|---|---|
| 6 | tablespoons butter |
| 1 | onion, chopped |
| 2½ | cups rice |
| 2 | cups orange juice and water combination (dilute to taste) |
| 2 | cups water |
| 1 | teaspoon grated orange rind |
| 2 | teaspoons salt |
| 1 | tablespoon parsley |

*Chicken*

| | |
|---|---|
| ¼ | cup butter |
| ½ | cup sliced almonds |
| 3 | whole chicken breasts, cut in half (6 serving pieces) |
| | Salt and pepper |
| 1 | cup water and orange juice combination |

1. In a large saucepan, sauté onion in butter until golden.
2. Add the rice and stir for a minute or two.
3. Add the remaining rice ingredients.
4. Bring to a boil, stir, cover and simmer for 20 minutes until rice is fluffy.
5. Leave covered until serving.
6. While rice is cooking, sauté almonds in ¼ cup butter in a large skillet. Remove almonds from skillet when golden brown, and set aside.
7. Rinse chicken breasts, and pat dry. Season with salt and pepper.
8. Brown (in same skillet that almonds were in) until a golden brown. This should take 15–20 minutes. Remove from skillet.
9. Deglaze skillet with 1 cup of orange juice. Boil and reduce by ½.
10. Fluff rice and place on a heated platter. Arrange chicken on top. Pour sauce over chicken and sprinkle with sautéed almonds. Garnish with orange slices.

**YIELD: 4–6 servings**
**PREPARATION TIME: 15 minutes**
**COOKING TIME: 25 minutes**

# CHICKEN AND ORZO SALAD

| | |
|---|---|
| ¾ | cup blanched sliced almonds |
| 1 | whole chicken breast |
| 1½–2 cups chicken broth | |
| 2 | cups orzo (after cooking) |
| 6 | tablespoons olive oil |
| 2 | tablespoons red wine vinegar |
| 2 | tablespoons lemon juice |
| | Dash Tabasco sauce |
| 3 | tablespoons combination of chives and parsley |
| | Salt and pepper |
| 1 | tablespoon minced red onion |
| 1 | tablespoon chopped parsley |
| | Spinach leaves and navel orange sections (optional) |

1. Toast almonds in a 425 degree oven for 5 minutes. Let cool.

2. In a covered pot, simmer chicken breast in broth to cover for 15 minutes. Let cool in liquid.

3. When cool, cut into bite-sized pieces.

4. Cook orzo according to package directions. Drain.

5. While pasta is still warm, toss with oil, vinegar, lemon juice, Tabasco, parsley, chives, salt and pepper to taste.

6. Add chicken, red onion, and almonds. Toss well and spoon onto a platter. Surround with spinach and orange sections tossed in a vinaigrette flavored with orange peel.

7. Sprinkle remaining parsley on top.

8. Refrigerate until serving or serve at room temperature.

**YIELD: 4 servings**
**PREPARATION TIME: 30 minutes**

# LENTIL AND
# BROWN RICE SALAD

A zesty main dish salad which can be prepared ahead of time. Garnish colorfully.

| | |
|---|---|
| 4 | cups minus 2 tablespoons water |
| | Salt |
| 1 | cup brown rice |
| 1 | cup minus 1 tablespoon lentils |
| 4 | scallions, thinly sliced |
| ½ | red onion, finely chopped |
| 2 | red or green peppers, finely chopped |
| 3 | tablespoons chopped parsley |
| 3 | tablespoons chopped raisins |
| 3 | tablespoons chopped nuts |

*Vinaigrette*

| | |
|---|---|
| ½ | teaspoon dry mustard |
| ½ | teaspoon granulated sugar (optional) |
| 6 | tablespoons red wine vinegar |
| | Salt and pepper |
| ¾ | cup olive oil or olive/vegetable oil mixture |

1. Bring 4 cups water to a boil. Add salt.
2. Rinse rice and lentils together in cold water.
3. Add to boiling water. Cover and reduce to a simmer. Cook 35 minutes.
4. While they are cooking, prepare a vinaigrette by combining mustard, sugar, vinegar, salt and pepper. Whisk in olive oil.
5. Transfer cooked rice and lentils to a large mixing bowl. While still warm toss in vinaigrette. Let cool.
6. Add remaining ingredients and toss.

YIELD: 6–8 servings
PREPARATION TIME: under 1 hour

VARIATIONS: Toss in any fresh vegetables, apples, or whatever appeals. Use the salad as a filling for hollowed tomatoes or stuffed peppers.

# THREE-CHEESE CREPES

Three-cheese crepes are equally at home at an elegant brunch or country supper. Although crepes have been much abused with fillings inappropriate to their nature, this rich, smooth filling gives the crepe the status it deserves. Serve with a crisp endive or watercress salad, along with orange slices marinated in champagne for a pleasing, balanced evening meal.

The basic crepes can be made well in advance and frozen with a sheet of waxed paper between each crepe. Or you can make them a day ahead and refrigerate.

*Basic Crepes*

| | |
|---|---|
| 2 | **eggs** |
| 2 | **tablespoons melted butter** |
| 1⅓ | **cups milk** |
| 1 | **cup flour** |
| | **Butter, as needed** |

*Sauce*

| | |
|---|---|
| 2 | **tablespoons butter** |
| 2 | **tablespoons flour** |
| ¾ | **cup chicken broth** |
| ¾ | **heavy cream** |
| ¼ | **cup grated Parmesan** |
| | **Salt and pepper, to taste** |

To prepare crepes:
1. Put eggs, butter, milk and flour in a blender or bowl of a food processor. Blend for 1 minute, stopping once to scrape down sides.

2. Butter a crepe pan or 6- to 8-inch skillet. Heat until just bubbling. Pour about ¼ cup of the batter into the pan. Immediately tilt the pan to spread the batter.

3. Cook until a light brown. Turn and cook other side briefly.

4. Repeat, adding more butter as needed.

5. Stack crepes, with a sheet of waxed paper between each. Keep covered.

Next, prepare sauce:
6. Melt butter in a medium-sized skillet. With a whisk stir in the flour, over low heat for 1 minute.

7. Pour in the broth and cream, stirring until smooth and slightly thickened, about 4 minutes.

8. Stir in Parmesan cheese, salt and pepper. Set aside.

*Filling*

| | |
|---|---|
| 1 | package (10 ounces) frozen chopped spinach, defrosted and drained |
| 1 | cup ricotta cheese |
| 1 | cup shredded mozzarella cheese |
| ½ | cup freshly grated Parmesan |
| | Salt and pepper, to taste |

*Topping*

Grated Parmesan cheese and bread crumbs

9. Have the spinach defrosting in a colander for the filling. Squeeze any remaining water out. Cook briefly in a dry pan, stirring continually to rid excess water. Heat through.

10. Preheat oven to 350 degrees.

11. Combine spinach with the remaining filling ingredients.

12. Put a few tablespoons sauce in the bottom of a baking dish that will hold a single layer of 10- to 12- folded crepes.

13. Spoon about ¼ cup of the filling into each crepe. Roll and place seam-side down in the baking dish. Continue until all the filling is used.

14. Pour the remaining sauce over crepes. Sprinkle with cheese and bread crumbs for topping.

15. Bake for 15 minutes or until bubbly.

YIELD: 4–6 servings
PREPARATION TIME: 40 minutes
BAKING TIME: 15 minutes

VARIATIONS: Crepe batter can have between ¼ to ⅓ cup of buckwheat or whole wheat flour in it.
Omit Parmesan cheese from the sauce and add some freshly grated nutmeg.

# Simply Elegant

# GARNISHES

To add drama, flair, whimsy or elegance to any dish, use garnishes, drawing on your personal palette of colors, moods and flavors.

The simplest touches are the most effective, I think. My preferences are garnishing with herbs or flowers. Individual sprigs of herbs centered on a whole roast, or a single sprig of watercress floating in soup add subtle elegance.

I use small bunches of wildflowers centered in tube cakes, blossoms surrounding a serving dish, a single violet on a serving of chocolate mousse. The possibilities are endless.

## FAVORITE GARNISHES

Herb wreaths

Whole sprigs of herbs

Violets

Molded herb butters

Stuffed cherry tomatoes

Fruit or vegetable
candle-holders

Rings of daisies
and red clover

Bouquets in middle of cake

Sugared rose petals
and pansy petals

Chive blossoms

Day lily blossoms

Nasturtium blossoms

Curls of citrus peel

# TARRAGON GRILLED SHRIMP

The more meals cooked outdoors in summer the better! Skewered seafood is especially nice because it is easy to transport. Marinate the shrimp in heavy plastic bags or containers that seal. At the beach or picnic site, thread on skewers and grill. Pile the shrimp, still skewered, on a platter.

| | |
|---|---|
| 2 | cloves garlic, split |
| ¼–⅓ | cup fresh tarragon leaves (or 1–2 tablespoons dried tarragon) |
| ⅓ | cup white wine |
| 1 | tablespoon lemon juice |
| ⅓ | cup olive oil |
| 1 | pound shrimp, shelled and deveined. Leave tails on. |

1. In a bowl, combine all ingredients, except shrimp.
2. Add shrimp, cover and marinate. This can be done 1–2 hours en route to a picnic or 4 or more hours in the refrigerator. Uncooked shrimp should be kept chilled as seafood deteriorates rapidly in warm weather.
3. Thread shrimp onto skewers.
4. Grill over hot coals for a few minutes on each side, 5–6 minutes total cooking time at most. Brush with marinade while cooking.

YIELD: about 6 skewers
PREPARATION TIME: 5 minutes
MARINATE: 3–4 hours
COOKING TIME: 6 minutes

VARIATIONS: Seasonal vegetables, such as tomatoes, zucchini, and onions can be threaded on the skewers and cooked with the shrimp. If you prefer your vegetables cooked longer, thread them on separate skewers as shrimp cook very quickly.

# GOUGÈRE WITH ARTICHOKE HEARTS AND FETA CHEESE

This is a very attractive dinner entree. The filling can be made in advance but the pastry should be made just prior to baking. It is fairly quick to prepare, so it still works well when entertaining.

*Filling*

| | |
|---|---|
| 3 | tablespoons butter |
| 1 | tablespoon olive oil |
| 1 | leek, white part only, chopped |
| 1 | tablespoon flour |
| | Salt and pepper |
| ½ | cup white wine |
| ½ | cup chicken broth |
| 1 | teaspoon tomato paste (optional) |
| 1 | tablespoon lemon juice |
| 8½ | ounces artichoke hearts, canned or frozen and thawed |
| 1 | tomato, peeled |
| 6–8 | black olives (optional) |
| 4 | ounces feta cheese |

1. To prepare the filling, heat the butter and olive oil in a large skillet.
2. Split white part of leek in half, carefully washing out the grit. Slice in thin slices.
3. Heat the leeks in butter until softened. Do not brown.
4. Stir in the flour, salt and pepper and continue cooking and stirring for 2 minutes.
5. Add wine, broth, tomato paste, and lemon juice. Bring to a boil and simmer 4 minutes. Remove from heat.
6. Cut peeled tomato in half and remove seeds with your fingers. Cut each half into 8 slices. Add to the leek mixture.
7. Halve each artichoke heart and add along with the optional olives. Set aside the filling and the feta cheese.
8. Preheat oven to 400 degrees.

*Pâte à Choux*

| | |
|---|---|
| 1 | cup sifted flour |
| | Salt and pepper to taste |
| 1 | cup water |
| ½ | cup butter, cut in 3 pieces |
| 4 | eggs, room temperature |
| 2 | tablespoons freshly grated Parmesan cheese |

*Topping*

| | |
|---|---|
| ⅓ | cup grated Parmesan cheese |
| | Parsley |

9. To prepare *pâte à choux*, sift flour, salt and pepper onto a paper plate or sheet of waxed paper.

10. Put water and butter in a large saucepan. Heat until the butter melts; then raise heat until the mixture boils.

11. Add flour *all at once* and stir continuously until the mixture draws away from the sides of the pan into a ball.

12. Remove pan from heat. Cool for 5 minutes.

13. Add eggs, one at a time, and beat very well after each addition with a wooden spoon.

14. Stir in Parmesan cheese.

15. Butter a 10- to 11-inch quiche or flan pan, or a baking dish.

16. Spoon pastry mixture into a ring around the edges of the baking dish.

17. Pour the filling into the middle of your ring. With the wooden spoon, push back *pâte à choux*, if it tends to slide toward the middle.

18. Break off the feta cheese into walnut-sized pieces; place throughout the filling.

19. Sprinkle Parmesan topping over all.

20. Bake for 35–40 minutes. *Gougère* will puff and brown, and filling will be bubbly when done.

21. Sprinkle with freshly snipped parsley and serve immediately.

YIELD: 6 servings
PREPARATION TIME: 35 minutes
BAKING TIME: 40 minutes

# GLAZED PORK TENDERLOIN WITH SAUCE CASSIS

Pork roasts are so satisfyingly easy to make, yet lend themselves to a quiet elegance. This one is particularly delicious served either hot or cold. The warm version is served with a sauce reminiscent of Kir, a Cassis-flavored drink. The cold roast makes for a pleasing picnic. Untie the roast at the picnic site, and serve with good French bread and sweet butter. When cooking, line a shallow roasting pan with foil to prevent the pan drippings, which are not used for the sauce, from burning.

| | |
|---|---|
| 2 | whole pork tenderloins, about ½–¾ pounds each |
| 1 | clove garlic, finely chopped |
| ¼ | cup red currant jelly |
| ¼ | teaspoon dry mustard |

*Sauce*

| | |
|---|---|
| ½ | cup white wine or dry vermouth |
| 2 | tablespoons Creme de Cassis |
| 2 | tablespoons cream (optional) |
| | Sprigs of fresh parsley and tarragon |
| 4 | black peppercorns |

1. Tie or have the butcher tie 2 pork tenderloins together, thin ends to wider ends, making one fairly even-sized roast.

2. Preheat oven to 375 degrees. Line a shallow roasting pan with foil.

3. Rub garlic over meat.

4. In a small saucepan, melt the currant jelly. Stir in the dry mustard to form a glaze.

5. Brush half the glaze over the meat. Set on a rack in roasting pan.

6. Put in the oven for 15 minutes. Then remove roast from oven, turn meat over and brush with remaining glaze. Return roast to oven.

7. Roast in oven for about 30–40 minutes more, or to an internal temperature of 165 degrees to 170 degrees (about 25–30 minutes per pound).

8. When done, remove roast from oven. If serving hot, allow to rest for 10 minutes before serving.

9. To serve with a sauce: Combine wine, Cassis, sprigs of parsley and tarragon, and peppercorns. Bring to a boil and reduce. Strain to remove herbs and peppercorns. Return to saucepan and stir in optional cream for a thick cream sauce.

10. Place roast on a heated platter. Remove strings and cut several slices, overlapping them on the platter. Garnish top of roast with additional sprigs of herbs. Carve remaining roast at the table, as needed. Spoon Cassis sauce over slices when serving.

11. To serve cold: Allow meat to cool. Keep tied. Wrap in foil and carry. Untie when slicing.

**YIELD: 5–6 servings**
**PREPARATION TIME: 15 minutes**
**ROASTING TIME: 45 minutes**

# SEAFOOD ROLLS
# WITH LEMON SAUCE

These seafood rolls are surprisingly simple to prepare. Delicately flavored, they make an impressive entree, especially when accompanied by colorful vegetables. Try a julienne of red, yellow and green peppers. Serve with a white Burgundy or Graves. For a very special evening, you may wish to serve smaller portions as appetizers.

*Seafood*

| | |
|---|---|
| ½ | pound (can be small frozen) shrimp, shelled and deveined |
| ¾ | pound salmon fillet, chopped |
| ¾ | pound haddock (or other dry white fish), cut in pieces |
| 3 | eggs |
| ½ | cup cream |
| 1 | tablespoon chopped parsley |
| | **Salt and pepper to taste** |

*Sauce*

| | |
|---|---|
| 6 | tablespoons white wine |
| 2 | tablespoons lemon juice |
| 2 | tablespoons chopped chives |
| 8 | tablespoons unsalted butter |
| ¾ | teaspoon grated lemon rind |

1. Chill the chopped salmon and shrimp in a bowl for 1½ hours.

2. In the bowl of a food processor, puree the haddock. Cover and chill for ½ hour.

3. Process the haddock puree with the eggs, cream, salt, and pepper until well combined. Chill for 1 hour.

4. Stir the shrimp, salmon and parsley gently into the fish puree.

5. Divide the mixture in half. Lay out 2 sheets of heavy duty plastic wrap. Roll each half of mixture into a log and wrap securely in the plastic wrap. Twist or tie the ends tightly. (Can prepare ahead to this point.)

6. Poach the wrapped rolls in simmering water for 15 minutes. Remove from water and let cool for 8–10 minutes.

| | |
|---|---|
| 1½ | teaspoons chopped fresh tarragon (½ teaspoon dried) |
| 2 | teaspoons minced parsley |

*Garnish*

| | |
|---|---|
| 1 | tablespoon chopped parsley |
| 2 | teaspoons chopped chives |

7. While seafood is cooling prepare the sauce. In a small saucepan, boil the wine, lemon juice, and chives, until reduced by half. Lower heat, whisk in the butter, 1 tablespoon at a time until incorporated. Stir in the lemon rind, tarragon and parsley. Add salt and pepper to taste.

8. Spoon some sauce on a warm serving platter. Unwrap the seafood rolls and place on the platter. Spoon remaining sauce on rolls and garnish with parsley and chives.

**YIELD: 4 servings**
**COOKING TIME: 45 minutes**
**REFRIGERATION TIME: 2 hours**
Can be prepared in advance except for final cooking.

# CHICKEN AND PUREE OF BROCCOLI WITH HOLLANDAISE SAUCE

Boneless chicken breasts are wrapped around broccoli puree, lightly fried to a crusty golden brown, and served with a sauce hollandaise.

| | |
|---|---|
| 4 | half breasts of chicken, boned and pounded to 1/16-inch thick |

*Puree*

| | |
|---|---|
| 1 | small head of broccoli, about 1¼ cups cooked |
| 1 | tablespoon butter |
| 1 | chopped shallot (optional) |
| 1 | tablespoon flour |
| 2 | tablespoons lemon juice |
| | Salt and pepper, to taste |

*Batter*

| | |
|---|---|
| 1 | egg, beaten |
| 1 | cup fresh bread crumbs, seasoned with salt, pepper and minced parsley |
| ½ | cup flour, more if needed |
| 1 | tablespoon milk |
| | Salt, pepper, nutmeg |
| | Vegetable oil |

1. Wash and trim the broccoli. Cut into pieces. Cook in boiling salted water until just tender; not mushy. Drain. Whirl in a food processor until pureed, or put through a food mill.

2. Melt the butter in a skillet. Sauté shallot until softened. Add flour; stir for 1 minute. Add lemon juice.

3. Stir in the broccoli puree. Add salt and pepper to taste. Set aside.

4. Beat the egg in a shallow bowl.

5. Lay pounded chicken on the counter. Sprinkle with salt and pepper. Put one quarter of the broccoli puree in the center of each chicken breast. Enclose filling by folding one long side over it. Then fold in each short side. Brush some of the egg on the unfolded long side and fold that over all. The result should be a neat rectangular packet.

6. Put seasoned bread crumbs and flour in separate shallow dishes. Pie plates work well.

7. Add milk, salt, pepper, and nutmeg to the beaten egg.

8. Coat each packet with flour, dip into egg mixture, then coat with bread crumbs.

9. Place on a wire rack over a baking sheet. Refrigerate for 2 hours.

10. Heat 2 inches of oil in a heavy skillet, until hot, about 365 degrees. Fry chicken, 2 packets at a time for 4 minutes, turning once.
11. Drain on paper towels.
12. Arrange on a platter. Drizzle some Hollandaise Sauce on each and briefly put under broiler to brown. Pass remaining sauce separately.

**YIELD: 4 servings**
**PREPARATION TIME: 45 minutes**
**REFRIGERATION TIME: 2 hours**

**VARIATIONS:** By changing the fillings you can vary this chicken. A filling of flavored butter turns it into a classic Chicken Kiev. Herbed cream cheese or sherried mushrooms are delicious. Omit the Hollandaise Sauce with these.

## HOLLANDAISE SAUCE

| | |
|---|---|
| 2 | egg yolks |
| 1½ | tablespoons lemon juice (or white wine vinegar) |
| 1 | teaspoon cream |
| | Salt |
| | Cayenne |
| ¼ | pound butter (1 stick) |

1. Put egg yolks and lemon juice in a small stainless steel bowl and beat with a wire whisk until combined.
2. Beat in cayenne, salt, and cream.
3. Place bowl in a skillet of hot water.
4. Beat over low heat until mixture thickens slightly.
5. Whisk in butter, a bit at a time, until melted and incorporated in sauce.

# COLD POACHED SALMON WITH WATERCRESS MAYONNAISE

A traditional offering that makes an intimate lunch when served on a shaded small table outdoors. This can make a lovely appetizer, or when served as an entree, a white burgundy, cucumber salad, French bread and sweet butter accompany it well.

| | |
|---|---|
| 2½ | pounds fresh center-cut salmon |
| 5 | cups liquid: fish stock with white wine, or white wine and water, or white wine and bottled clam juice. |
| 1 | medium onion, coarsely chopped |
| 1 | carrot, coarsely chopped |
| 1 | rib celery including leaves, coarsely chopped |
| | Parsley, bay leaf, tarragon, tied together in cheesecloth |

1. Combine all ingredients except salmon in an enamel casserole. Simmer, covered, for ½ hour.
2. Wash and dry the salmon. Sprinkle inside with salt and pepper. Wrap in cheesecloth.
3. Gently place the salmon in the simmering liquid.
4. Raise heat and boil for 2 minutes.
5. Remove the pan from the heat. Allow the fish to cool in the broth. Drain and refrigerate the salmon.
6. Remove from refrigerator 15 minutes before serving.
7. Prepare watercress mayonnaise. Serve on chilled platter garnished with watercress sprigs.

**YIELD: 4 servings**
**PREPARATION TIME: 30 minutes**

# WATERCRESS MAYONNAISE

| | |
|---|---|
| 1 | egg yolk |
| 1 | tablespoon Dijon-style mustard |
| 1 | tablespoon lemon juice or white wine vinegar |
| | Salt and pepper to taste |
| 1 | cup oil (combination of olive and vegetable) |
| ½ | bunch watercress, stems removed |
| 2 | tablespoons fresh chopped chives |

1. Beat egg yolk, mustard, lemon juice, salt and pepper in a mixing bowl with a wire whisk.

2. In a *very* slow stream, add the oil while continuing to beat.

3. Rinse, dry thoroughly, and chop the watercress. Fold it into the mayonnaise with the chives.

4. Reseason with salt and pepper as needed.

# BAKED RED SNAPPER IN LOUISIANA SAUCE

There is nothing quite so striking as a beautifully presented whole fish. This one, baked in an incredible Creole sauce with eggplant, will dazzle your guests. Excellent for entertaining, the sauce can be prepared a day ahead of time leaving you free to enjoy your friends, while the fish bakes. Spinach noodles round out this meal nicely. I use a whole fish because it looks so beautiful on a platter garnished with lemon slices, but if you prefer, remove the head, tail, or serve fish fillets.

| | |
|---|---|
| 1 | whole red snapper, absolutely fresh |

*Sauce*

| | |
|---|---|
| ¼ | cup olive oil |
| 2 | cups chopped onion |
| 1 | cup chopped red or green pepper |
| 1 | cup chopped celery |
| 2 | cloves garlic, minced |
| 2¼ | pounds tomatoes, canned |
| 6 | ounces tomato paste |
| | Salt and pepper to taste |
| 1 | tablespoon Worcestershire sauce |
| 1 | strip lemon rind |
| 2 | cloves |

1. Sauté onion, peppers, celery and garlic in the oil until the onion is translucent.

2. Add the tomatoes and remaining ingredients except for the eggplant. Simmer for 10 minutes.

3. Stir in the eggplant and cook gently for an additional 20 minutes.

4. Preheat oven to 325 degrees.

5. Spoon some of the sauce in the bottom of an oblong or fish-shaped baking dish. Place the fish on the sauce and put the remaining sauce inside the cavity, on top of, and around the fish.

6. Bake for about 45 minutes. (10 minutes for each inch of thickness at the thickest part of the fish).

**YIELD:** 4 servings
**COOKING TIME:** 30 minutes
**BAKING TIME:** about 45 minutes

| | |
|---|---|
| ½ | teaspoon sugar |
| ½ | teaspoon thyme |
| ½ | teaspoon rosemary |
| 1 | bay leaf |
| 1 | drop Tabasco |
| ¼ | cup chopped parsley |
| 1 | medium-sized eggplant, coarsely chopped and drained |

**VARIATIONS:** Prepare extra sauce and freeze it in small batches. This Creole Sauce is excellent also with baked shrimp and other fish.

# THE NARROWS FISH STEW

The Narrows is the stretch of ocean in Maine that we visit in the summer. This particular fish stew is simple and elegant when served in large shallow bowls along with a salad of Belgium endive and a walnut vinaigrette. Pass whole crusty baguettes for guests to break off large chunks for dipping in the rich broth.

| | |
|---|---|
| 2 | tablespoons olive oil |
| 2 | onions, chopped |
| 4 | cloves garlic, minced |
| 1 | rib of celery, chopped |
| 2 | tomatoes, peeled and chopped (or 8-ounce can of plum tomatoes) |
| 2 | cups dry white wine |
| 3 | cups fish stock (or 2 cups clam juice and 1 cup water) |
| 2 | tablespoons chopped parsley |
| 1 | bay leaf |
| 1 | 2-inch strip of orange peel (optional) |
| 1½ | pounds available white fish, cut in 1-inch pieces (cod, haddock, bass, monkfish) |
| ½ | pound scallops |
| 10–15 | mussels (well-cleaned in several changes of water) |
| ¼ | cup white wine |
| 1 | teaspoon tarragon |

1. Lightly saute onions, garlic and celery in olive oil until soft, but not browned.

2. Add tomatoes, 2 cups wine and stock. Stir in parsley, bay leaf and orange peel. Simmer for 30 minutes.

3. Simmer the mussels in an additional ¼ cup of wine for approximately 6 minutes. Remove with a slotted spoon. Discard any unopened mussels. Remove mussels from shells. Strain cooking broth through cheesecloth.

4. Stir the white fish and scallops into the tomato-wine sauce, and add the tarragon, peppercorns, and Pernod.

5. Cook until the fish and scallops turn opaque, about 4 or 5 minutes. Do not overcook or fish will toughen.

6. Add mussels and strained mussel broth to the stew.

7. To prepare the sauce, beat the garlic, egg yolk and a pinch of salt together in a separate bowl. Very slowly add olive oil, almost a drop at a time, while whisking continuously until incorporated.

| 4–6 | crushed peppercorns |
|---|---|
| 1 | tablespoon Pernod (optional) |

*Sauce*

| 1 | clove garlic, minced |
|---|---|
| 1 | egg yolk |
| | Pinch salt |
| ¼ | cup olive oil |

8. A tablespoon of this sauce may be dolloped on top of each serving, or beat 2 tablespoons of the hot stew liquid into the sauce and then add all the sauce to the stew pot. Stir until well incorporated and season to taste with salt and pepper.

YIELD: 8 servings
PREPARATION TIME: 45 minutes

# RAGOUT OF VEAL AND ARTICHOKES

Despite a long list of ingredients this is quickly put together and shares the advantage of most stews: the flavors improve the next day.

| | |
|---|---|
| | Olive oil |
| 3 | onions, chopped |
| 3 | cloves garlic, minced |
| 2½–3 | pounds veal stew meat, cut in 1½-inch to 2-inch cubes |
| 3 | tablespoons flour |
| 1½ | cups beef broth |
| ¾–1 | cup white wine |
| | Juice of 1 lemon |
| 2 | tablespoons tomato paste |
| 1 | bay leaf |
| ½ | teaspoon rosemary |
| | Pinch thyme |
| | Freshly ground black pepper |
| 1 | package frozen artichoke hearts, partially defrosted |
| ¾ | pound mushrooms, sliced |
| ¼ | cup black olives (optional) |
| | Grated lemon peel (optional) |
| ¼ | cup finely cut parsley |

1. Heat 2 tablespoons olive oil in a large skillet. Sauté the onions and garlic until translucent. Transfer to a 5-quart Dutch oven or enamel stove-top casserole with a lid.

2. Add another 2 tablespoons olive oil to the large skillet and brown the veal, a few pieces at a time, over medium-high heat. Add to Dutch oven. Continue browning veal, adding more oil as needed.

3. Lower heat under skillet. Add 2 tablespoons oil and the flour, stirring to make a paste. Add broth, wine, and the juice of 1 lemon. Stir up brown bits from the bottom of the pan. Add bay leaf, rosemary, thyme, pepper and tomato paste. Simmer for 5 minutes.

4. Pour this sauce over the veal in the Dutch oven. Cover and cook for 1 hour.

5. Uncover and continue cooking for 50 more minutes, stirring frequently.

6. Add the sliced mushrooms to the skillet. Cover and cook over medium-high heat for 2 minutes; uncover and stir until liquid has evaporated.

7. Add the sautéed mushrooms, along with the artichoke hearts, black olives and lemon peel to the Dutch oven. Simmer for 10 more minutes.

8. Ten minutes before serving, add the parsley to the ragout, and reheat.

YIELD: 8 servings
PREPARATION TIME: 25 minutes
COOKING TIME: 2 hours 15 minutes

# SHRIMP AND POTATO SALAD

Prepare this salad in advance, as it needs to marinate at least 4 hours. Honeydew melon and lime complement it well. For serving, spoon the salad in the center of a platter, and surround with blanched, whole marinated green beans sprinkled with shallots.

| | |
|---|---|
| 1½ | pounds medium-sized shrimp, cooked and peeled |
| 8 | small red potatoes |
| 3 | shallots, finely chopped |
| | Salt and pepper |
| 3 | tablespoons fresh tarragon chopped, or 2½ teaspoons dried |
| 1 | cup dry vermouth or white wine |
| 2 | tablespoons Cognac |
| 3 | tablespoons lemon juice |
| | Dash Tabasco |
| ½ | cup olive oil |

1. Wash potatoes, but do not peel. Boil until just tender, not mushy. Slice in ¼-inch slices.
2. While still warm, put a generous layer of potatoes in a large bowl. Sprinkle the layer with some of the shallots, salt, pepper, tarragon, and then some vermouth.
3. Cover this with a layering of shrimp. The shrimp will make a sparser layer than the potatoes. Repeat sprinkling with shallots, etc.
4. Continue layering and sprinkling until the shrimp and potatoes are used.
5. Cover and refrigerate for 4 hours, or overnight.
6. Just prior to serving, combine Cognac, lemon juice, salt, pepper, Tabasco and olive oil.
7. Pour over salad and toss.

YIELD: 6 servings
PREPARATION TIME: 30 minutes

# TOURNEDOS AND ARTICHOKES IN BÉARNAISE SAUCE

Tournedos are cut from the thinner end of a fillet. They are about 2 inches in diameter and 1-inch thick. Their tenderness and petite size make them an elegant steak.

They are best when simply sautéed and garnished with flair.

| | |
|---|---|
| 4 | tournedos |
| 1 | clove garlic, split |
| | Salt and pepper |
| 3 | tablespoons butter (2 tablespoons plus 1 tablespoon) |
| 4 | rounds of French or crustless white bread |
| 4 | fresh artichoke bottoms, cooked and trimmed |

1. Melt 2 tablespoons butter in a skillet. Season meat with salt and pepper; rub with garlic.
2. When butter is hot, add meat. Cook over medium-high heat until brown. Turn meat, lower heat, and sauté 6–7 minutes until rare or medium-rare. Do not overcook.
3. Remove meat from pan.
4. Add remaining 1 tablespoon butter to skillet, and brown bread on both sides.
5. Place browned bread on 4 warmed plates. Place meat atop each bread. Place artichoke bottom over meat. Fill each bottom with Bernaise sauce, allowing sauce to spill over and surround meat. Garnish with parsley and serve immediately.

YIELD: 4 servings
PREPARATION TIME: 30 minutes

# BÉARNAISE SAUCE

| | |
|---|---|
| ¼ | cup white wine vinegar or tarragon vinegar |
| ¼ | cup white wine or vermouth |
| 2 | teaspoons chopped shallots or scallions |
| 1 | teaspoon tarragon |
| | Salt and pepper |
| 2 | egg yolks |
| ¼ | pound butter (1 stick) |
| | Few drops lemon juice |
| | Minced parsley |

1. In a small saucepan, bring vinegar, wine, shallots, tarragon, salt and pepper to a boil, and reduce to about 2 tablespoons. Cool slightly.
2. Beat in yolks until smooth
3. Put mixture into a small stainless steel bowl and place in a skillet with about 1 inch of simmering water in it.
4. Whisk sauce until it begins to thicken.
5. Beat in butter, bit by bit.
6. Before serving, add a few drops of lemon juice and parsley.

**YIELD:** ½ cup
**PREPARATION TIME:** 20 minutes

# CRUMBED CHICKEN IN WINE SAUCE

A rich and delicious offering. Ideal for entertaining, most of the preparations can be done early in the day or the night before. Even the sauce can be made ahead of time and reheated with sour cream just before serving. Wild rice, Sautéed Cherry Tomatoes (see page 102), and small whole green beans quickly simmered in chicken broth add color and texture to the meal.

*Chicken*

| | |
|---|---|
| 8–10 | chicken breast halves |
| | Salt and pepper |
| ⅔ | cup sour cream |
| 6 | tablespoons butter, melted |
| 2 | cups fresh bread crumbs |

*Sauce*

| | |
|---|---|
| ½ | cup dry white wine |
| 1 | onion, chopped |
| 6 | peppercorns |
| 1 | bay leaf |
| 1 | strip lemon rind |
| 1 | tablespoon mixed fresh herbs (thyme, sage, marjoram, tarragon), or 1 teaspoon dried herbs |
| ⅔ | cup sour cream |

1. Rinse and pat chicken dry with a paper towel. Season with salt and pepper.
2. Arrange pieces in a single layer in a shallow dish. Spread with sour cream.
3. Cover and refrigerate 4 hours or overnight. Turn once or twice, respreading sour cream, as you turn.
4. Preheat oven to 375 degrees.
5. Combine melted butter and bread crumbs.
6. Coat chicken well on all sides with this mixture.
7. Arrange in baking dish and cover with foil.
8. Bake until browned, 30–35 minutes, turning once or twice.
9. While chicken is baking (or in advance), begin sauce. Put wine, onion, bay leaf, peppercorns, herbs and lemon rind in a small saucepan. Cover and bring to a boil. Simmer gently for 5 minutes.
10. Uncover and continue boil until sauce is reduced by half.
11. Strain. (After straining, sauce can be refrigerated until serving or proceed.)
12. When ready to serve, stir ⅔ cup sour cream into sauce and add salt to taste. Heat gently; do not boil. Serve sauce in gravy boat to be ladled over chicken.

**YIELD: 6–8 servings**
**PREPARATION TIME: Under ½ hour**
**MARINATING AND BAKING TIME: 5 hours or more**

# PRETTY MARSH MUSSELS WITH ANGEL HAIR PASTA

Rumor has it that the mussels from Pretty Marsh are the best in the world. Whatever your source for fresh mussels, here is a dish that makes a lovely first course, and a total (but wonderful) indulgence as a main course.

| | |
|---|---|
| 1 | tablespoon butter |
| 1 | tablespoon flour |
| ½ | cup white wine |
| ½ | cup fish stock or bottled clam juice |
| 4 | pounds mussels |
| 1 | shallot, chopped |
| 1 | sprig parsley |
| | Freshly ground pepper |
| ½ | cup white wine, or vermouth, or hard cider and water |
| 1 | egg yolk |
| 3 | tablespoons cream |
| 1 | pound angel hair pasta, cooked |
| | Parsley |

1. To begin sauce, melt butter in a skillet. Stir in flour; cook for 2 minutes. Add ½ cup wine and stock. Simmer 10–15 minutes.

2. Meanwhile, debeard and scrub mussels well in several changes of water. Discard any that are open.

3. Put mussels, shallot, parsley, pepper and another ½ cup wine in a large pot. Cover and bring to a boil. Simmer for about 6 minutes. Shake pan to encourage shells to open.

4. Remove mussels with a slotted spoon. Set aside.

5. Strain broth through cheesecloth, if necessary. Add to simmered sauce and cook for 10 minutes more.

6. Remove sauce from heat. Beat together yolk and cream; very slowly pour into sauce while stirring.

7. Divide cooked pasta among 4 heated plates. Remove mussels from shells and place on top of pasta.

8. Pour sauce over mussels. Garnish with parsley or watercress and serve hot.

YIELD: 6 main course servings; 8–10 first course servings
PREPARATION TIME: 40 minutes

# CHICKEN MARSALA WITH PROSCUITINI

This dish, and delicious variations of it, is easy enough to cook for a family weeknight meal and special enough for entertaining. Its versatility makes it fun to prepare. Serve it with buttered orzo, garlic bread and a spinach salad.

| | |
|---|---|
| 2 | large chicken breasts, halved and boned |
| | Flour |
| ¼ | cup olive oil |
| ¼ | cup butter |
| ⅓ | cup chicken broth |
| ⅓ | cup Marsala |
| 4 | slices proscuitini or prosciutto |
| 4 | slices fontina or Swiss cheese |

1. Lightly dust boned chicken breasts with flour. Place between 2 sheets of waxed paper and flatten slightly.
2. Heat olive oil in a large skillet and sauté chicken breasts, 4 minutes per side, until brown. Remove from pan.
3. Discard most of the olive oil. Add butter, broth and Marsala. Stir over moderate heat until the butter is melted. Return chicken to the pan.
4. Place proscuitini on chicken. Place a slice of cheese over all.
5. Cover the pan and continue cooking until cheese has softened and is bubbly.
6. Remove chicken and arrange on a heated platter. Turn up heat and reduce sauce to thicken. Spoon sauce over the chicken.

**YIELD:** 4 servings
**COOKING TIME:** 30 minutes

VARIATIONS: Add 10–12 sliced mushrooms to the butter before adding broth and Marsala. Sauté briefly.
Substitute 8 spears of asparagus (cooked) for the proscuitini.

# LINGUINE IN HERBED ARTICHOKE SAUCE

The flavors of tomatoes, cream and wine delicately blend with mushrooms and artichokes in this subtle sauce. Most of this sauce can be made ahead of time. Prepare through adding the artichokes. Set aside. Before serving, cook the pasta and heat the cream with the sauce. Toss all together in a large glass serving bowl and serve with garlic bread.

| | |
|---|---|
| 12–16 | ounces linguine or similar light pasta |
| 1 | tablespoon butter |
| 2 | tablespoons olive oil |
| 10 | ounces mushrooms, wiped clean and sliced |
| 1 | onion, chopped |
| 2 | cloves garlic, minced |
| ½ | cup white wine |
| 1 | cup chicken broth |
| | Salt and pepper to taste |
| 1 | tablespoon fresh basil or 1 teaspoon dried |
| | Pinch rosemary (optional) |
| 2 | tablespoons chopped parsley |
| 2 | tablespoons tomato paste |
| 1 | 10-ounce package frozen artichoke hearts, prepared according to directions, and quartered |
| ½ | cup heavy cream |

1. Heat butter and oil in a skillet. Add mushrooms, onion and garlic. Sauté over gentle heat until tender; garlic and onion should not brown.

2. Raise heat. Add wine and broth. Stir until mixture comes to a boil. Stir in herbs and tomato paste. Simmer for about 5 minutes, stirring occasionally.

3. Add artichoke hearts. Cook gently for a few minutes more.

4. Cook pasta. Drain and put in a heated bowl or platter.

5. Stir the cream into the sauce. Heat to almost boiling.

6. Toss sauce with pasta. Serve immediately with hot garlic bread.

YIELD: 4–6 servings
PREPARATION TIME: 10 minutes

# SKEWERED GINGER CHICKEN

Chicken marinated in a lime and ginger sauce, then skewered with red onion, cherry tomatoes, and green peppers. These kabobs make a wonderful main course, or arrange on smaller wooden skewers for a fanciful hors d'oeuvre to serve at dusk.

| | |
|---|---|
| 2 | whole chicken breasts (boneless, or bone yourself) |
| 1½ | teaspoons freshly grated ginger |
| | Juice of 1 lime |
| | Grated peel of 1 lime |
| 1 | clove garlic, minced |
| 1 | shallot (or small onion), finely chopped |
| ½ | cup vegetable oil |
| 2 | drops Tabasco sauce |
| 10 | cherry tomatoes, halved |
| 1 | large green pepper, cut in 1-inch squares |
| 1 | large red onion, cut in thin wedges |

1. Slice chicken away from the bone, and cut into 1-inch cubes or squares.

2. In a wide, shallow bowl, combine ginger, lime juice, rind, garlic, shallot, oil and Tabasco.

3. Add chicken squares; toss to coat. Marinate in the refrigerator 3 hours or more, or at room temperature for 2 hours.

4. Thread chicken, tomatoes, pepper and onion wedge on skewers in whatever sequence you fancy. Reserve marinade.

5. Allow chicken to drain by propping skewers over a long enough dish to catch the drippings.

6. Light outdoor grill or fire. When coals turn gray, grill meat 6 inches above the heat source. Brush with reserved marinade. Turn after a few minutes and cook a few minutes more, about 3–4 minutes per side.

YIELD: 6
MARINATE: 3 or more hours
PREPARATION TIME: 15 minutes

# MARYLAND CRAB STEW

This is thick, rich, and delicious. Beautiful when served in large shallow warmed bowls.

| | |
|---|---|
| 1 | pound fresh crab meat |
| 2 | tablespoons butter |
| | Salt |
| | Freshly ground pepper |
| 2 | cups milk |
| 2 | cups half-and-half |
| | Drop of Tabasco |
| 1 | teaspoon Worcestershire sauce |
| 6 | tablespoons port or sherry |
| 4 | slices lemon |
| | Chopped parsley |

1. Combine crab, butter, salt, pepper and milk in a saucepan.
2. Simmer for 10 minutes.
3. Add half-and-half and seasonings. Bring to near boil but do not allow to boil. Stir gently.
4. Remove from heat and add port.
5. Serve in warmed soup bowls with a lemon slice floating in each bowl. Sprinkle with parsley.

**YIELD: 4 servings**
**PREPARATION TIME: 15 minutes**

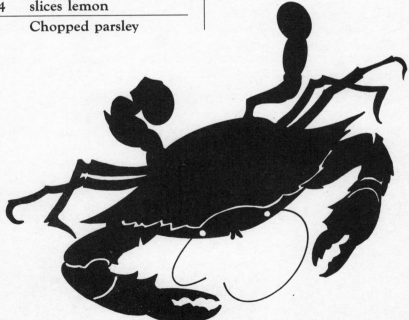

# TWO ROAST CHICKENS

Most of us imagine eating roast chicken in winter, with perhaps stuffing, gravy, vegetables, maybe biscuits—indeed, a warm traditional meal.

A well-roasted chicken need not be part of a heavy or wintery dinner. It can be juicy, tender, flavorful, and very light. Rather than filling the chickens with stuffing, select sprigs of herbs from the garden. The flavors will subtly permeate the chicken. What a lovely summer meal . . . chicken roasted in the early cool of day, delicately flavored with basil, chives or tarragon, and served later in the day, with bread, spinach salad and chilled wine or lemony iced tea.

## ROASTING CHICKEN

There are many approaches to roasting a chicken—breast side up, down or both; rack or not, truss or not; covered with foil at beginning, at end of roasting or not at all; oven temperature 325 degrees all the way to 450 degrees; basted with butter, water or not basted at all. Use any technique which yields good results for you. The important thing is not to overcook it—dried out chicken is a disaster. The meat is finished cooking when the thigh joint moves easily, or the meat feels soft when squeezed. Juices will run out clear, not pink.

In the following recipes, I use a 350 degree oven for about 22 minutes per pound. I baste frequently. Flavor the meat by filling the cavity with salt, pepper, onions, garlic, parsley, and available herbs or fruits.

## LEMON ROASTED CHICKEN

| | |
|---|---|
| | 2½–3½ pound roasting chicken |
| | Salt and pepper |
| 1 | lemon, halved |
| 1 | clove garlic |
| ½ | onion or 1 shallot |
| | Salt and pepper |
| | Sprig of parsley |

1. Preheat oven to 350 degrees.
2. Prepare chicken by cutting the fat from its cavity and removing the giblets. Rinse in cool water and dry with paper towels, inside and out.
3. Salt and pepper inside of chicken. Squeeze in juice of ½ lemon and then place the lemon in the cavity. Also add onion or shallot, and sprigs of parsley and thyme.

**Sprig of thyme
(optional)**

**Butter or oil**

*Gravy*

**1    tablespoon flour**

**1¼  cups chicken broth**

**¼    cup white wine or
      vermouth**

**1    tablespoon lemon juice**

4. Rub outside of chicken with salt, pepper, and butter or oil.

5. Place meat, breast side down, in a shallow pan. Do not use a rack.

6. Baste after 20 minutes with accumulated pan juices or a lemon juice and water mixture.

7. After 10 more minutes, baste again and turn the chicken breast side up for the remaining basting and cooking.

8. Roast for 20–25 minutes per pound. The thigh joint should move easily up and down, and the juices run clear when done.

9. When chicken is ready, remove to a platter. Serve when meat cools to room temperature (most flavorful) or refrigerate for serving later. Allow to return to room temperature before serving.

10. For serving warm with gravy: Pour off all but 2 tablespoons of drippings in pan. Heat them (in roaster) on top of stove. Add 1 tablespoon flour and stir with a wire whisk. Stir in broth and wine. Bring to a boil and simmer until slightly reduced and thickened. Squeeze in remaining lemon juice. Add salt and pepper to taste.

**YIELD: 4–6 servings**
**PREPARATION TIME: 15 minutes**
**ROASTING TIME: About 1 hour**

# BASIL CHICKEN

Make this at the end of summer, when you are tired of pesto and your fresh basil supply is still plentiful. Be sure to serve this with garden fresh tomatoes and basil, drizzled with olive oil, and generously seasoned with salt and pepper.

| | |
|---|---|
| 2½–3 pound roasting chicken | |
| 1 | small bunch chives, snipped or 1 shallot |
| 1 | generous bunch fresh basil |
| 1 | clove garlic |
| | Olive oil |
| | Salt and pepper |

1. Preheat oven to 350 degrees.
2. Remove fat from cavity. Rinse chicken in cool water and pat dry with paper towels, inside and out.
3. Salt and pepper cavity. Add the chives or shallot, and many basil leaves. Reserve 8 leaves.
4. Rub olive oil and salt over outside of bird.
5. Place chicken, breast side down, in a shallow pan. Do not use a rack. Baste after 20 minutes with pan juices. After 10 more minutes, baste again and remove from oven.
6. Turn chicken breast side up. Arrange basil leaves in a pattern over breast. Affix these with a thin coating of olive oil.
7. Return to oven and continue roasting and basting until done, about 20–25 minutes per pound or until thigh joint moves easily, and juices run clear.
8. Place chicken on platter. Serve warm or at room temperature with pan juices.

YIELD: 4–6 servings
PREPARATION TIME: 15 minutes
COOKING TIME: About 1 hour

# Around the Meal

# SPRING LUNCH

On those gorgeous spring days, when melted cheese sandwiches are too reminiscent of colder times, but the garden is not yet for the picking, try this between-season lunch.

| | |
|---|---|
| 2 | small whole wheat pitas, cut in half |
| ½ | cucumber, peeled, sliced lengthwise, and seeded with a spoon |
| 1 | avocado |
| | Juice of ½ lemon |
| ½ | small red onion |
| ½ | cup grated cheddar cheese |

1. Chop into small dice the cucumber and avocado.
2. Stir in the juice of ½ lemon.
3. Finely chop the red onion, and stir in.
4. Dice cheese and mix in.
5. Add additional lemon juice, salt and pepper to taste.
6. Fill pita halves and TAKE WALKING!

VARIATIONS: This recipe is obviously for adapting. Substitute or add nuts, mushrooms, olives, sprouts, apples, whatever you have on hand, whatever appeals.

# BUTTERNUT SQUASH BISQUE

We always welcome November with this soup. The color is the same gentle gold of autumn fields. Have a basketful of apples on the table, serve bowls of this warm soup, and settle in to celebrate the quiet coziness that is November.

This soup may be made ahead of time. Refrigerate the puree. Reheat before serving; then add the cream.

| | |
|---|---|
| 1 | small butternut squash, about 1–1¼ pounds |
| 2 | green apples, peeled, cored, and coarsely chopped |
| 1 | small onion, chopped |
| ¼–½ | teaspoon curry powder |
| 6 | cups rich chicken stock or broth |
| 2 | slices bread, cubed |
| 1 | teaspoon salt |
| ¼ | teaspoon pepper |
| ¼ | cup heavy cream |

1. Halve and seed the squash.
2. Put the squash, along with the remaining ingredients, except the cream, in a large soup pot.
3. Simmer for 45 minutes.
4. Remove squash. Separate the peel from the squash and return squash to the pot.
5. Puree in a blender or food processor.
6. Reheat the puree; add cream.
7. Serve piping hot in warm bowls.

YIELD: 4–6 servings
PREPARATION TIME: 10 minutes
COOKING TIME: 50 minutes

VARIATIONS: Omit chicken broth and use a vegetable broth for a vegetarian soup.
The cream can be omitted for a lovely, yet lighter, soup.
Try marjoram or rosemary instead of the curry.

# VERMONT CHEESE SOUP WITH HERBED CROUTONS

We are really partial to a good farmhouse cheddar in our family, and Vermont Cheese Soup showcases its robust flavor. Cheese soup always seems just right—easy and very warming on a wintery night.

Quick to make, this soup is better prepared right before serving. Sharp cheeses (aged) melt better in cooking—younger cheeses become gummy. Remember to warm soup bowls before filling, and garnish generously with Herbed Croutons or topping of your choice.

| | |
|---|---|
| 2 | tablespoons butter |
| 2 | tablespoons finely chopped onion |
| 1 | clove garlic, minced |
| 2 | tablespoons flour |
| 1 | cup chicken broth |
| 5 | cups milk |
| 2 | cups grated aged cheddar cheese, packed tightly |
| ½ | teaspoon Worcestershire sauce |
| | Pinch dry mustard and salt |
| | Pepper |
| | Paprika |

1. Melt butter in a soup pot. Add onion and garlic, stirring until golden.
2. Add flour; whisk for a minute or two.
3. Slowly pour in the broth, and then milk. Continue stirring until slightly thickened.
4. Add cheese, Worcestershire sauce, and mustard, stirring in 1 direction.
5. When cheese is melted, add salt and pepper to taste.
6. Ladle into heated bowls, sprinkle dash of paprika over each serving, and garnish with the topping of your fancy, or pass bowls of varied garnishes.

YIELD: 4 servings
PREPARATION TIME: 15 minutes
COOKING TIME: 15 minutes

*Garnish*

**Choose from:**

**Crumbled bacon**

**Herbed croutons**

**Red peppers**

**Toasted almonds**

**Tomato slices**

**VARIATIONS:** The chicken broth can be omitted, or you can substitute with tomato juice. Skim milk also works well. Garnishes are limited only by imagination: try popcorn, broccoli pieces, fresh basil leaves.

# HERBED CROUTONS

Herbed croutons are delicious, using a variety of breads and herbs.
Cube stale bread; sauté quickly in butter flavored with garlic and herbs. Store in tightly closed jars in the refrigerator.
Croutons can also be prepared by drying bread cubes in a 350 degree oven for 5 minutes. Then, brush with melted butter or oil that has been flavored with garlic and herbs. Continue baking until bread cubes are dried and golden brown, about 3 minutes more.

# CREAM OF WATERCRESS SOUP

The tartness of watercress combines with rich cream in this spring-time soup. It is easy to prepare and can be done ahead of time.

Sprigs of watercress poking through French bread form a pretty floating garnish. If new violets are available to you, float them with the watercress. The colors are delightful.

| | |
|---|---|
| 2 | tablespoons butter |
| 2 | tablespoons flour |
| 4 | cups watercress (about 2 bunches) carefully rinsed |
| 6 | cups chicken broth or 4 cans, undiluted |
| | Pepper |
| 1 | cup heavy cream |

*Garnish*

| | |
|---|---|
| 8 | slices French bread |
| 16 | sprigs of watercress |

1. In the bowl of a food processor or blender (in half batches), combine butter, flour, watercress and broth. Process for about 1 minute.

2. Refrigerate, covered, until just before serving.

3. Transfer to a large saucepan. Bring to a boil, stirring. Add pepper and cream, stirring for a few minutes longer.

4. Ladle into warmed soup bowls. Poke stems of watercress through thin slices of French bread. Float one in each bowl.

**YIELD:** 8 servings
**PREPARATION TIME:** 15 minutes

# BLACK BEAN SOUP

A distinctive soup enhanced by the tartness of lemon. It epitomizes country elegance, especially when served in fine china bowls on a candlelit evening. Leave plenty of time for the long slow simmer essential to the success of this soup.

| | |
|---|---|
| 3 | tablespoons oil |
| 1 | small clove garlic, minced |
| 1 | onion, finely chopped |
| 1 | rib celery, finely chopped |
| 1½ | cups black beans, washed and picked through |
| 6 | cups chicken broth |
| | Salt and pepper to taste |
| 2 | tablespoons chopped parsley |
| ⅔ | cup lemon juice |
| 2 | tablespoons sherry |

*Garnish*

Lemon slices

Parsley

Yogurt or sour cream (optional)

1. Heat oil in a soup pot and sauté garlic, onion and celery until tender.
2. Add broth and beans. Bring to a boil, cover, and simmer over low heat for 3 hours.
3. Whirl soup in a food processor or blender, along with salt, pepper and parsley. This will take a few batches. Return puree to the soup pot.
4. Add lemon juice and sherry. Reheat soup. Adjust consistency by adding more broth if needed (this is usually served as a rather thick soup).
5. Ladle hot soup into warmed soup bowls. Garnish by floating lemon slices with a sprinkling of parsley in each bowl or with a dollop of yogurt and parsley.

YIELD: 6 servings
PREPARATION TIME: 20 minutes
COOKING TIME: 3 hours

**VARIATIONS:** For a meatless soup use a good vegetable broth instead of chicken broth. Finely chopped hard-boiled egg can be used as the garnish.

# WINE CONSOMMÉ

This versatile consommé is ideal when unexpected guests drop in, for packing in thermoses for woodland walks, and an unabashed favorite with cross-country skiers. Don't let its simplicity put you off; this one is both easy and good.

| | |
|---|---|
| 3½–4 | cups beef broth (preferably your own, or canned) |
| 1 | cup red wine |
| 2–3 | teaspoons lemon juice |
| 1 | sprig parsley, finely chopped |

1. Heat broth and wine just to the point of boil.
2. Reduce heat and cook for 2 minutes.
3. Prior to serving, add lemon juice and parsley.
4. Serve in heated mugs or pour into a thermos for picnics.

**YIELD: 4–5 servings**
**PREPARATION TIME: 5 minutes**

# AUBERGINE APPETIZER

Guests rarely realize this is eggplant. Because it takes different garnishes so well, eggplant allows for a creative hand in presentation which is half the fun and challenge of hors d'oeuvres anyway. Dollop yogurt or arrange chopped parsley and red onion over the top. Garnish and serve as a dip for crudités or with whole wheat pita triangles. Try it also as a side dish with grilled lamb.

A blender or processor is needed for this dish. Plan 45 minutes for baking the eggplant, but after that it is quickly prepared. The water in eggplant has a bitter taste, and recipes often call for salting and draining for this reason. In this recipe, after the eggplant bakes, the bitterness can be squeezed out.

| | |
|---|---|
| 1 | medium-sized eggplant, 1–1¼ pounds |
| 1–2 | cloves garlic |
| | Juice of ½ lemon |
| | Dash Tabasco sauce |
| ¼ | cup olive oil |
| | Salt, pepper |
| 2–3 | tablespoons chopped parsley |

*Optional Garnishes*

| | |
|---|---|
| 2 | small whole wheat pitas, cut in quarters |
| | Chopped red onion |
| | Chopped parsley |
| | Chopped dill |
| | Finely chopped egg |
| | Black olives |
| | Cherry tomatoes |
| | Yogurt |

1. Preheat oven to 400 degrees.
2. Bake whole eggplant on a baking sheet for 45 minutes, until tender.
3. When cool, peel off the skin. Squeeze the eggplant to drain juices. Split and remove seed bundles.
4. Add eggplant, garlic, Tabasco, and lemon juice to a blender or food processor. Process until smooth.
5. With the motor still running, add the olive oil in a slow stream.
6. Transfer to a serving bowl. Season with salt, pepper and parsley. Mix through.
7. Cut pitas into triangles. Cover eggplant with additional chopped parsley and set pitas point side up around the dish. Garnish as desired.

PREPARATION TIME: 10 minutes
BAKING TIME: 45 minutes

# MARINATED ASPARAGUS

Ah, asparagus . . . We wait and await springtime, crocus and hepatica bloom, and our hearts leap, but when the asparagus push up we know spring is really here!

Garden fresh asparagus should be picked as close to cooking time as possible for flavor and sweetness are lost in the time lapse. If you are without an asparagus bed, buy spears with tight buds. To maintain freshness, store the spears in the refrigerator with the stalks standing in water.

| | |
|---|---|
| 1 | pound asparagus |
| | Pinch salt |
| 1 | shallot, finely chopped |
| 1 | tablespoon red wine vinegar, or balsamic vinegar |
| 1 | teaspoon lemon juice |
| ½ | teaspoon Dijon-style mustard |
| | Salt and pepper |
| 3 | tablespoons olive oil |

1. Bring 2 inches of water to a boil in a skillet large enough to lay asparagus flat. Add a pinch of salt.

2. Wash asparagus in cold water. Break off the tough base of each. Remove scales if they are large or sandy.

3. Place spears in the boiling water. Quickly return water to a boil, then uncover and gently simmer.

4. Cook for 5–7 minutes. Do not overcook! Asparagus should be slightly crisp.

5. Drain. Place in an oval dish to marinate.

6. Chop the shallot. Put in a small bowl. Add and stir the vinegar, lemon juice, mustard, salt and pepper. Whisk in olive oil.

7. Pour over warm asparagus. Allow to marinate at room temperature until cool; then refrigerate until serving. Return to room temperature before serving.

8. Serve on individual salad plates, spooning vinaigrette and shallots over each serving or lay spears on a white oval platter and top with marinade.

YIELD: 4 first course servings or 2 servings for real asparagus fans
PREPARATION TIME: 10 minutes
COOKING TIME: 5 minutes

# PISTOU

*Pistou* is traditionally used as a rich addition to soups. It is a thick mayonnaise-like sauce, stirred into soups or spooned on top. I think it especially delicious on tomato-based vegetable, bean, or fish soups, but it is also excellent on poached or grilled meats and fish.

| | |
|---|---|
| 2 | slices bacon, chopped |
| ½ | cup water |
| 2 | egg yolks |
| 2 | cloves garlic, minced |
| 1 | tablespoon fresh basil (1 teaspoon dried) |
| 2 | teaspoons chopped parsley |
| ⅓ | cup freshly grated Parmesan cheese |
| 2 | tablespoons olive oil |

1. Simmer bacon in water for 5 minutes. Drain.
2. Put yolks, garlic, basil and parsley into a blender or food processor. Blend until pureed.
3. Transfer to a mixing bowl. Stir in Parmesan cheese.
4. Beat in olive oil, drop by drop, until well combined.

YIELD: ⅔ cup
PREPARATION TIME: 10 minutes

# COLD BRAISED LEEKS IN CRÈME FRAÎCHE

We all know leeks as the delicious and subtle flavoring for soups and stews. They are also incredibly versatile; I encourage you to try them in different ways. Cream cheese, leeks, and ham combine for a wonderful main course soup. Leeks can be creamed and gratineed for a side dish. Braised leeks, allowed to cool in flavorful sauces, make a lovely first course, such as leeks *à la greque* or the following braised leeks in a *crème fraîche*. Both the leeks and sauce can be prepared ahead of time and combined just prior to serving.

| | |
|---|---|
| 8 | leeks, trimmed of all but 1 inch of the green and well rinsed |
| 2 | tablespoons butter |
| ½ | teaspoon salt |
| 1 | cup *crème fraîche* or sour cream |
| ½ | teaspoon curry |
| 1 | small clove garlic, finely minced |
| 1 | teaspoon grated horseradish |
| 2 | tablespoons cider vinegar |
| | Chives and chive blossoms (optional garnish) |

1. Combine leeks, butter and salt in a covered casserole. Add water to cover.

2. Bring to a boil, lower heat, and simmer until barely tender. Test with a fork. Cooking time will vary according to size of the leeks, but do not overcook.

3. Drain leeks well. Refrigerate until serving.

4. In a small bowl, combine remaining ingredients and stir well.

5. Arrange leeks on a serving platter or individual salad plates. Pour the sauce over them.

6. Garnish with snipped chives and chive blossoms.

YIELD: 4 servings
PREPARATION TIME: 15 minutes
COOKING TIME: 10 minutes

# CRÈME FRAÎCHE

*Crème fraîche* is a distinctively tart soured cream, widely used in French cooking. It can be used as a base for salad dressings, sauces for vegetables and soups, and dolloped on fruits and berries, either sweetened or plain.

You can now buy a commercial *crème fraîche* at some markets, but it is easy to prepare at home and will keep about 2 weeks, refrigerated.

| | |
|---|---|
| **4** | **cups heavy cream** |
| **1** | **cup buttermilk** |

1. Combine liquids.
2. Pour into a large jar with cover. Wrap in a dish towel and set in a warm place, away from drafts, for 24 hours. The cream will thicken and have a slightly acidic taste.
3. Store in the refrigerator.

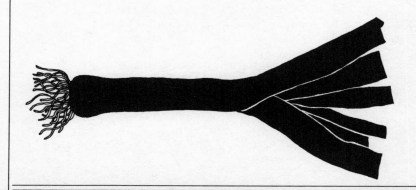

# A GALAXY OF ONIONS

Five different onions add flavor and character to this impressive dish. It is a terrific complement to the traditional dishes of Thanksgiving. In fact, this dish is an immediate favorite whenever it is served.

It can be prepared in advance, except the final baking, a helpful feature in the frenzy of holiday cooking or a company dinner.

| | |
|---|---|
| 3–4 | tablespoons butter |
| ½ | pound shallots, whole or halved if particularly large |
| 6–8 | leeks, white part only, split and well rinsed, cut in 1-inch rounds (not smaller) |
| 1 | large yellow onion, halved lengthwise and sliced in large wedges |
| 1 | large red onion, halved lengthwise and sliced in large wedges |
| 2 | cloves garlic, minced |
| 12 | pearl onions |
| 2 | cups heavy cream |
| | Salt and pepper |
| | Grated nutmeg |
| ¼ | cup minced parsley |
| 3 | tablespoons fresh bread crumbs |

1. Melt butter in large skillet or Dutch oven.
2. Add the garlic and the onions, except the pearl onions.
3. Toss gently over low heat, until onions soften, about 20–30 minutes. Do not brown.
4. While onions are cooking, drop pearl onions into boiling water and simmer for 5 minutes. Drain. Make a slit across root end; onions will slip out of their skins. Add the parboiled pearl onions to the cooked onions.
5. Add the cream to the onions. Bring to a boil and simmer until cream is reduced and thickened, about 10–15 minutes.
6. Season to taste with salt and pepper. Stir in the parsley.
7. Preheat oven to 475 degrees.
8. Spoon into a buttered shallow baking dish.
9. Sprinkle with bread crumbs.
10. Bake 15 minutes until golden.

**YIELD: 8–10 servings**
**PREPARATION TIME: 50 minutes**
**BAKING TIME: 15 minutes**

# GOLDEN POTATO PUREE

I just *love* this recipe—the color, the texture, the taste. It is delicious and interesting enough for company, available and easy enough for anytime. Try it . . . you'll see.

| | |
|---|---|
| 1 | small- to medium-sized rutabaga, peeled and cut into eighths |
| 3 | medium-sized potatoes, peeled and cut into halves |
| 6 | tablespoons butter |
| 1 | medium-sized onion, chopped fine |
| 1 | teaspoon salt |
| ¾ | teaspoon paprika |
| | Black pepper, to taste |

1. Cook both vegetables in separate pots of boiling water until fork tender.
2. While they are cooking, melt butter in a small skillet. Add onions and cook gently until translucent. Do not brown. Add salt, pepper, and paprika.
3. Drain potatoes and rutabagas. Put through a food mill together with onions.
4. Serve in a warmed vegetable dish. Sprinkle with added paprika if desired.

**YIELD:** 6 servings
**PREPARATION TIME:** 30 minutes

# SAUTÉED CHERRY TOMATOES

A vegetable side dish full of promise. Sautéed Cherry Tomatoes are an attractive and colorful addition to any meal. Remarkably good and quick to prepare, as well.

| | |
|---|---|
| 2 | cups cherry tomatoes, washed and dried |
| 2–3 | tablespoons unsalted butter |
| ½ | teaspoon salt |
| ½ | teaspoon granulated sugar |
| 1 | tablespoon fresh basil leaves, finely chopped |
| 1 | tablespoon chopped parsley |
| | Pepper to taste |

1. Heat butter in a pan.
2. Add salt, sugar, basil and parsley. Stir briefly.
3. Add whole tomatoes all at once, shaking pan to coat tomatoes with butter.
4. Cook, occasionally shaking pan, until warm but not mushy, about 3 minutes.
5. Serve warm garnished with sprigs of basil.

YIELD: 4 servings
PREPARATION TIME: 5 minutes

# SAUERKRAUT AND APPLES

A simple, satisfying dish served either as a side dish or the entree. For light suppers, serve with boiled potatoes, rye bread, and cold beer or cider.

| | |
|---|---|
| 2 | pounds sauerkraut, rinsed (preferably fresh-packed, not canned) |
| 1 | cup water |
| ¼ | pound bacon |
| 1 | onion, coarsely chopped |
| 2 | apples, chopped |
| ½ | teaspoon caraway seeds |

1. Simmer sauerkraut in water for 10 minutes.
2. Cook bacon in large, heavy skillet. As fat renders, add onions and apples. Stir and continue cooking until onion is tender.
3. Drain sauerkraut. Toss with bacon mixture and caraway seeds.
4. Serve hot on a pewter plate surrounded by boiled potatoes.

YIELD: 4–6 servings
PREPARATION TIME: 5 minutes
COOKING TIME: 10 minutes

# SALAD DRESSINGS

Salads are, I think, a matter of personal taste, imagination, and creativity. In summer with its almost limitless bounty, salads can be as diverse and imaginative as your spirit. In winter, we have to dig further, often raiding the pantry in lieu of the garden to give salads balance—both nutritional and culinary.

To me, the key to salad making is in a light touch: dressings that enhance, rather than mask; vegetables simply prepared, revealing their individual textures and flavors, never served icy cold; stereotypes avoided by serving the salad when most appropriate—before, during or after the main course (if not as the main course)—in fact, salads play a key role in the orchestration of the meal for fullest impact.

My favorite salad? Boston lettuce tossed with a simple vinaigrette.

## FAVORITE VINAIGRETTE

| | |
|---|---|
| 1 | clove garlic, minced |
| ¼ | teaspoon salt |
| 2 | tablespoons red wine vinegar |
| 7 | tablespoons olive oil (or part olive oil, part vegetable oil) |
| | Freshly ground pepper, to taste |

1. Make a paste of the garlic and salt.
2. Add vinegar and pepper.
3. Whisk in oil.

## IN-THE-BOWL DRESSING

1. Rub garlic clove over salad bowl.
2. Add washed, dry greens.
3. Spoon olive oil over leaves and mix.
4. Add a little vinegar. Toss to coat greens. Sprinkle with salt and pepper. Mix well.

# HONEY-SOY VINAIGRETTE

A light vinaigrette that is especially good tossed with any combination of blanched winter vegetables—carrots, broccoli, peppers, water chestnuts, celery—for a chilled salad or side dish. Add left-over meat, and turn this into a main dish winter salad.

| | |
|---|---|
| ⅓ | cup water |
| ⅓ | cup peanut or corn oil |
| ⅓ | cup cider vinegar |
| 2 | tablespoons light soy sauce |
| 2 | tablespoons minced scallions |
| 2 | teaspoons honey |
| ¼ | teaspoon ground ginger |

1. Combine ingredients in a small jar with a tight fitting lid.
2. Shake well to mix.

# SOUR CREAM DRESSING

| | |
|---|---|
| ½ | cup sour cream or yogurt (half of this can be mayonnaise) |
| 2 | tablespoons vinegar |
| 2 | teaspoons granulated sugar |
| 1 | clove garlic, minced |
| ½ | teaspoon salt |
| ½ | teaspoon dry mustard |
| ¼ | cup milk |

1. Combine all ingredients.
2. Refrigerate 4 hours or overnight.

# LEMON-DIJON DRESSING

Juice of ½ lemon
(approximately 2
tablespoons)

½ teaspoon Dijon-style
mustard

⅓ cup oil

Freshly ground pepper,
to taste

1. Whisk together lemon juice and mustard.
2. Continue whisking while adding oil in a slow stream.
3. Add pepper to taste.

# WARM BACON DRESSING

Excellent for a winter salad of spinach and flavored croutons.

4 slices bacon, cut in
1-inch pieces

2 teaspoons brown sugar

2 tablespoons cider
vinegar

Freshly ground black
pepper

1. Fry bacon. Do not drain.
2. Add brown sugar. Stir; then add vinegar. Cook for 1 minute.
3. Season with pepper to taste.
4. Spoon bacon and dressing over greens. Serve immediately.

# ABOUT HERBS

Fresh herbs add a lot to cooking. I always try to have at least basil, parsley, chives and tarragon growing. Herbs do fine in flowerpots on windowsills, patios, fire escapes. They're an inspiration in themselves on a tired-feeling day. Pick all summer from the bottom leaves. When harvesting in the fall, cut only the top ⅓ of the plant, tie in small bunches, and hang in a cool dark place. Quick drying preserves flavor and color.

- One teaspoon of a dried herb is equal to a tablespoon of fresh.
- Try layering basil leaves in olive oil instead of drying them. Tarragon dries well but also makes delicious vinegar; soak leaves in cider or white wine vinegar for 2 weeks. Make some in empty small wine bottles and give as presents.
- Fresh herbs delightfully change salad dressing. Add chopped basil, chives, chervil, oregano, savory or tarragon to the vinegar, while making a vinaigrette. Experiment.
- Classic vinaigrette proportions are 3 parts oil to 1 part vinegar. This can be varied to taste increasing the oil. Olive oils vary; again experiment. Use ½ vegetable, peanut or walnut oil for a lighter dressing. Add herbs, garlic, mustard, lemon juice and always use freshly ground pepper.

# TOMATOES

GROW tomatoes! Even if you don't garden, grow tomatoes; on city roof or fire escape, grow tomatoes; hidden in suburban shrubbery, grow tomatoes!

In Vermont we are limited to when we can eat fresh tomatoes but not to how much . . .

- Best, simply sliced. Sprinkle with salt, pepper and fresh basil, drizzle with a good olive oil and vinegar, vary by adding chopped red onions, shallots or parsley.
- Toss coarsely chopped tomatoes, cucumbers and red onions with vinaigrette.
- Tomato sandwiches: Sliced tomatoes on French bread, topped with olive oil, salt, pepper and basil. Only after many of these sandwiches, do we waiver and add cheese, sometimes melted over the top.
- Thickly slice green tomatoes, dip in cornmeal, and sauté in butter. Brown sugar and cream can be added to the pan drippings, after tomatoes are cooked tender.
- Fresh tomato soup: Cook carrots, onions, green or red peppers until soft. Briefly cook tomatoes and puree all through a food mill.

# HUNGARIAN RICE SALAD

There is probably little that is Hungarian about this salad except it is colorful and reminds me of my Grandmother. "It's the gypsy in you," she used to tell me, when as a child I insisted on wearing bright colors, especially red. This rice dish complements a variety of summer meals. Use only garden fresh tomatoes. For advance preparation, make the dressing and refrigerate it. Combine the rice, tomatoes, and onions ahead, but toss with the dressing just prior to serving.

| | |
|---|---|
| 2–2½ | cups cooked rice |
| 4–5 | tomatoes, coarsely cut in bite-sized pieces |
| 1 | onion, finely chopped |
| | Salt and pepper to taste |
| ¼ | cup oil |
| ¼ | cup red wine vinegar |
| 1–2 | tablespoons granulated sugar |
| 4 | tablespoons chopped parsley and/or snipped chives |
| | Pinch salt and pepper |

1. Combine rice, tomatoes and onion. Add salt and pepper to taste.
2. Mix oil, vinegar, sugar, salt and pepper together in a small jar.
3. Pour over rice salad, and mix well.
4. Sprinkle parsley or chives over all.

YIELD: 5–6 servings
PREPARATION TIME: Under 15 minutes

# GREEN BEAN
# AND NEW POTATO SALAD

A fresh tasting salad, both lighter and zestier than the traditional. The beans give a nice crunch and together with new potatoes fairly shout summer is here! Serve this salad still slightly warm or cooled to room temperature. It is best when made ahead of time, allowing the flavors to meld. If it is made early in the day, it may be refrigerated, but allow sufficient time to return to room temperature before serving.

| | |
|---|---|
| 3 | tablespoons red wine vinegar |
| 5–6 | tablespoons olive oil |
| 1 | clove garlic, minced |
| ½ | teaspoon salt |
| | Freshly ground black pepper |
| 4 | new or small red potatoes |
| ¾ | pound small green beans |
| 2 | tablespoons chopped red onion (or shallots) |
| 4 | tablespoons chopped parsley |

1. Combine vinegar, oil, garlic, salt and pepper in a medium-sized serving bowl.
2. Wash potatoes; do not peel. Cook until just tender; the time will vary according to the size of your potatoes. Do not overcook.
3. Drain and cool potatoes until they can be handled. They can be slipped out of their skins, or leave the skins on. Cut in ⅛-inch slices.
4. Toss the warm potatoes in the vinaigrette.
5. Wash the beans and break off the tips. Steam briefly until just crisp tender. Rinse under cold water. Pat dry.
6. Toss the beans with the potatoes.
7. Sprinkle parsley and red onion, over all.

**YIELD: 4–6 servings**
**PREPARATION TIME: 30 minutes plus cooling**

# MOLDED GAZPACHO SALAD

A light summer lunch, serve with fresh chives mixed in cottage cheese, leaf lettuce, and rolls with sweet butter.

| | |
|---|---|
| 1 | envelope unflavored gelatin |
| 1½ | cups tomato vegetable juice |
| 2 | tablespoons red wine vinegar or cider vinegar |
| 1 | small clove garlic, minced |
| 1 | tomato, chopped |
| 1 | green or red pepper, seeded and chopped |
| 1 | medium-sized cucumber, peeled, seeded and chopped |
| ½ | medium-sized red or yellow onion chopped |
| 2 | tablespoons chopped chives |
| | Salt and pepper |
| | Parsley |

1. Soften gelatin in ¼ cup juice. Heat 1 cup juice and stir in gelatin to dissolve.
2. Add vinegar, and remaining ¼ cup juice to hot mixture.
3. Stir in garlic, tomato (and its juices), pepper, cucumber, onion, and chives.
4. Season to taste with salt and pepper.
5. Pour into a single quart mold. Chill until firm, at least several hours.
6. Turn out onto a platter lined with lettuce. Garnish with parsley.

YIELD: 6 servings
PREPARATION TIME: 25 minutes
REFRIGERATION TIME: 3 hours or longer

# MARINATED CHICK PEA SALAD

My children have always loved this salad. It is easily made with ingredients on hand—on hand I suppose only if you keep cans of chick peas on your shelf, and we always do.

Chick pea salad can be easily doubled or more. Prepare it ahead of time; the taste improves as the flavors marry. It is particularly good with grilled meats. Serve on a bed of radicchio leaves and garnish with black olives cured in garlic, oil and herbs.

| | |
|---|---|
| 1 | 16-ounce can chick peas, drained |
| 1 | clove garlic, minced |
| ½ | small red onion, finely chopped (or substitute a shallot) |
| 2–4 | tablespoons chopped parsley |
| 3 | tablespoons red wine vinegar or lemon juice (or combination of both) |
| 3 | tablespoons olive oil |
| | Salt and pepper, to taste |

1. Drain chick peas.
2. In a separate bowl, combine remaining ingredients and whisk until well blended.
3. Add chick peas and toss.
4. Let marinate for 30 minutes or more.

YIELD: 6 servings
PREPARATION TIME: 5 minutes
MARINATE: 30 minutes minimum

# WINTER FRUIT BOWL

Winter fruit admittedly leaves something to be desired. Yet, it's that very plain quality that makes it ideal for combining with special flavorings and sauces. Here a fruit bowl made up of whatever you can readily find in your supermarket becomes inspired with the tartness and tang of *crème fraiche*.

| | |
|---|---|
| 1 | cup *crème fraiche* (see page 99), or sour cream |
| 3 | tablespoons powdered sugar |
| 2 | tablespoons Amaretto |
| 1 | teaspoon vanilla extract |
| 1–2 | teaspoons lemon juice |
| | Bananas, sliced |
| | Seedless grapes, halved |
| | Clementines, peeled and in sections (or other seedless orange) |
| | Apples, cored and sliced |
| | Strawberries, if available |
| | Blueberries, if available |

1. Combine *crème fraiche*, sugar, Amaretto and extract in a small bowl. Mix well.
2. Cover and chill until ready to assemble.
3. Gently toss fruits together with the lemon juice.
4. Arrange in a glass compote or other serving dish.
5. Top with sauce.

**PREPARATION TIME: 20 minutes**

# COUNTRY BAKED APPLES

Country foods can be so versatile. Baked apples are a good example of a homey family dessert—easily made company special. Serve on a pretty plate with softly whipped Calvados-flavored cream alongside.

| | |
|---|---|
| 2 | baking apples, Rome Beauty or Cortland |
| | Lemon juice |
| | Heavy cream |

*Filling #1*

| | |
|---|---|
| 2 | tablespoons butter |
| 3 | tablespoons brown sugar |
| 1 | teaspoon cinnamon |
| ⅓ | cup oats |
| 2 | tablespoons butter (reserve) |

*Filling #2*

| | |
|---|---|
| 3 | tablespoons good apricot preserves |
| ¼ | teaspoon lemon peel |
| 1 | tablespoon Calvados or brandy |
| 1 | tablespoon sliced almonds |
| 2 | tablespoons butter (reserve) |

1. Preheat oven to 400 degrees.
2. Wash and dry apples. Peel ⅓ way down the apple. Core from the stem end, being careful not to pierce through the bottom. A spoon can be used to dig out and increase the cavity size.
3. Rub a small amount of lemon juice over cut surfaces to prevent discoloration.
4. Combine filling ingredients for filling #1 or #2, reserving last 2 tablespoons butter in each recipe.
5. Spoon prepared filling inside each apple.
6. Place apples in an ovenproof dish. Divide butter; place on top of the apples.
7. Add 1 inch water to the dish. Bake uncovered for 45 minutes or until tender.
8. Serve each apple on an individual plate. Pass a pitcher of heavy cream or softly whipped cream flavored with Calvados and powdered sugar.

YIELD: 2 apples per filling
PREPARATION TIME: 15 minutes
BAKING TIME: 45 minutes

**VARIATION:** Wrap the fancy baked apples in squares of puff pastry and bake, as directed.

# Desserts:
# Plain & Fancy

# A STRAWBERRY LEMONADE AFTERNOON

*White sheep, white sheep*
*On a blue hill,*
*When the winds stops*
*You all stand still;*
*When the wind blows*
*You walk away slow;*
*White sheep, white sheep,*
*Where do you go?*

CHRISTINA G. ROSSETTI

I share this drink despite its obvious simplicity. The flavor, color, appearance and mood this Strawberry Lemonade creates are quite special.

**Lemonade (preferably freshly squeezed, but frozen concentrate will do)**

6–8 **very ripe strawberries**

1. On a gorgeous summer afternoon, with the bluest sky and whitest clouds, drop the strawberries into a glass pitcher of cold lemonade.

2. Watch the berries slowly tint the lemonade a delicate pink.

3. Spread a cloth under a tree; pour icey glasses of lemonade for any neighboring children you can gather, and read poems together as the clouds and afternoon drift along.

# A LUSCIOUS LEMON CREAM

We love this dessert. It is incredibly simple and simply elegant. Serve it in a crystal bowl or individual champagne glasses. It has become a tradition for our fanciest picnic on the 4th of July. We garnish it with strawberries and notice how quickly they disappear as friends dip them into the lemon cream. Pack extra berries for dipping.

| | |
|---|---|
| 1 | pint heavy cream |
| ½ | cup granulated sugar |
| 4 | lemons, the juice and grated zests |
| 2 | tablespoons condensed milk |

*Garnish*
**Strawberries, blueberries, raspberries**

1. Combine all ingredients in a large, chilled mixing bowl.
2. Beat until very thick.
3. Divide among glasses or heap into a bowl.
4. Chill until serving.
5. Garnish with berries.

YIELD: 8 servings
PREPARATION TIME: 10 minutes

**VARIATIONS:** Change fruit garnishes according to the freshest available: raspberries, blueberries, blackberries, etc. Fill bottom of crystal bowl with berries and then heap on lemon cream and garnish. Delicious also as a filling in a meringue pie crust shell.

# RASPBERRIES
# IN CRÈME ANGLAISE

Fill a parfait dish with raspberries and swirl on *crème anglaise*; the combination is absolutely luscious. *Crème anglaise* adds enchantment to a summer brunch, and exquisite richness to any dinner dessert.

*Crème anglaise* is a custard sauce which enhances a variety of desserts with its subtle richness. It may be served warm or cold. When warm, it is a delicate counterpoint over cold chocolate mousse or a frozen dessert. When cold, it is best served over cakes, fruits, and trifles.

This is a basic recipe, definitely worth adding to your repertoire. The only trick in preparation is to keep the heat low—when heat is too high, the egg yolks will curdle.

**Raspberries, divided among serving dishes**

*Crème anglaise*

| | |
|---|---|
| 6 | egg yolks |
| ⅓ | cup sugar |
| ⅛ | teaspoon salt |
| 2 | cups half-and-half or milk, scalded |
| 1½ | teaspoons vanilla extract |
| 1 | tablespoon Grand Marnier, Cointreau, or sherry |

1. Beat egg yolks, sugar and salt in a heavy saucepan until light and fluffy.
2. While stirring, gradually add scalded milk to the yolk mixture.
3. Cook over a medium-low heat, stirring with a wooden spoon for about 10 minutes. The mixture will coat the back of a metal spoon when done. Do not boil!
4. Let cool a bit; then add vanilla and liqueur.
5. Stir occasionally to prevent film from forming.
6. Serve warm or cover and chill.
7. To serve with raspberries: spoon ¼ cup of cooled sauce over berries in individual serving glasses or bowls.

YIELD: about 3 cups
PREPARATION TIME: 15–20 minutes
COOKING TIME: 10 minutes

**VARIATIONS:** Variations seem infinite. The sauce is delicious over any fruits and berries, and many cakes.
A favorite dessert is chocolate crepes rolled around chocolate mousse and then frozen. Serve them with warm *crème anglaise*.

# RENATE'S SWEDISH CAKE

A quickly prepared, buttery cake that Renate introduced to Wild Farm. Carry it in the pan to a breakfast picnic, or serve it with iced tea on the porch. The top is macaroon-like and needs no additional topping.

| | |
|---|---|
| 3 | eggs |
| 1½ | cups granulated sugar |
| 1½ | sticks butter, melted |
| 1½ | cups flour |

*Optional flavorings to taste:*
   **Orange peel**
   **Cardamon**
   **Nutmeg**
   **Nuts**

1. Preheat oven to 350 degrees.
2. Beat 3 eggs with the sugar.
3. Add melted butter, flour and optional flavorings.
4. Pour batter into a single 9-inch round cake pan.
5. Bake for 40 minutes. Check cake. When it is a light brown, turn off oven and let cake cool in oven.
6. To serve, cut in thin wedges.

**PREPARATION TIME: 15 minutes**
**BAKING TIME: 40 minutes**

# CHOCOLATE ALMOND TORTE

A dark and very chocolatey creation for those times when only chocolate (and the richer the better) will do. Two frostings are given— one a cocoa whipped cream, the other a chocolate butter cream. Each is very good; choose whichever will complete your perfect chocolate temptation.

*Cake*

| | |
|---|---|
| 4 | ounces sweet baking chocolate |
| 2 | ounces unsweetened baking chocolate |
| ½ | cup butter (1 stick) |
| 6 | eggs, separated |
| ⅔ | cup granulated sugar |
| 3 | tablespoons flour |
| 1 | teaspoon vanilla extract |
| 1½ | cups ground almonds |

1. Preheat oven to 325 degrees.
2. Butter an 8- or 9-inch springform pan.
3. Melt the chocolate in a double boiler or small stainless bowl over a pan of simmering water. Let cool.
4. Cream the butter until light and fluffy.
5. Gradually add the cooled chocolate to the butter and continue beating.
6. Add 5 yolks (reserve 6th for icing or other use) one at a time, beating well after each addition.
7. Gradually add the sugar while beating.
8. Stir in the flour and vanilla.
9. Fold in the almonds.
10. Beat whites of the 6 eggs until stiff. Stir a spoonful of whites into batter to lighten, then carefully fold in remaining whites.
11. Spoon into the prepared pan.
12. Bake for 35–40 minutes. Cake should begin to separate from the sides of the pan when done.
13. Allow the cake to cool in the pan on a rack.
14. Frost with either of the following icings or a rum-flavored whipped cream.

**YIELD:** 12 servings
**PREPARATION TIME:** 35 minutes
**BAKING TIME:** 40 minutes

*Icing #1*

| | |
|---|---|
| **4** | **tablespoons unsalted butter** |
| **1** | **cup powdered sugar** |
| **1** | **egg yolk** |
| **1** | **tablespoon cocoa** |
| **1½** | **teaspoons rum** |

1. Cream butter with the egg yolk.
2. Beat in the sugar and cocoa.
3. Stir in rum and beat until fluffy.
4. Spread on top of the cooled cake.
5. Decorate with sliced or whole almonds.
6. Refrigerate ½ hour or until serving.

**PREPARATION TIME: 10 minutes**
**REFRIGERATION TIME: 30 minutes**

*Icing #2*

| | |
|---|---|
| **½** | **cup heavy cream** |
| **2** | **ounces semisweet chocolate** |
| **3** | **tablespoons powdered sugar** |
| **1** | **teaspoon vanilla extract** |

1. Combine cream and chocolate in saucepan.
2. Cook until chocolate melts and mixture begins to boil.
3. Stir and refrigerate until lukewarm.
4. Beat. Gradually add sugar and vanilla while continuing to beat.
5. Spread on top of cake and refrigerate until serving.

**PREPARATION TIME: 10 minutes**
**REFRIGERATION TIME: 10 minutes**

# WHIPPED CREAM CAKE WITH ALMOND CUSTARD FILLING

Whipped cream is used instead of shortening in this cake. The flavor is delicate and best topped with a white frosting and a subtle filling such as the almond custard given here. Try flavored whipped creams, apricot or chestnut fillings. For summer birthday parties, surround this cake with a ring of day lilies.

*Cake*

| | |
|---|---|
| 2 | cups flour |
| 1⅓ | cups granulated sugar |
| 2¾ | teaspoons baking powder |
| ½ | teaspoon salt |
| 1 | cup heavy cream |
| 3 | egg whites |
| ¼ | teaspoon salt |
| ½ | cup water |
| 1 | teaspoon vanilla extract |
| ½ | teaspoon almond extract |

1. Preheat oven to 350 degrees. Butter 2 8-inch layer cake pans.
2. Sift together dry ingredients.
3. Beat the heavy cream until stiff.
4. Clean and dry the beaters. Beat egg whites until foamy; add salt and continue beating until stiff.
5. With a rubber spatula, combine the whipped cream and egg whites. Fold in water and extracts.
6. Fold the dry ingredients into the whipped cream mixture a third at a time.
7. Spoon the batter into the greased pans.
8. Bake for 30 minutes or until the cake begins to pull away from the sides of the pan and a tester comes out clean.
9. Allow cakes to cool for 10 minutes on a rack. Turn out of pans to continue cooling.
10. To prepare glaze, melt apricot preserves and Amaretto in a small pan. Brush the glaze on the top of each layer while still slightly warm. Let cool completely, while preparing the filling.

*Glaze*

| ¼ | **cup apricot preserves** |
|---|---|
| 2 | **tablespoons Amaretto or brandy** |

*Almond custard filling*

| ½ | **cup granulated sugar** |
|---|---|
| ½ | **cup sour cream** |
| 1 | **teaspoon cornstarch** |
| 1 | **beaten egg yolk (reserve white for frosting)** |
| ½ | **cup ground almonds** |
| ½ | **teaspoon vanilla extract or Amaretto** |

*Frosting*

| 1 | **egg white** |
|---|---|
| ¾ | **cup granulated sugar** |
| 2½ | **tablespoons water** |
|  | **Cream of tartar** |
| 1 | **teaspoon light corn syrup** |
| 1 | **teaspoon vanilla extract** |

11. Combine sugar, sour cream and cornstarch in a saucepan. Stir over very low heat. Pour over the beaten egg yolk. Return to low heat, and stir until thickened. Stir in almonds. When cool, add vanilla or Amaretto.

12. Spread the custard on 1 cake layer over the glaze. Place the second layer on top, glaze side up.

13. To prepare the frosting, measure all ingredients except vanilla into top of double boiler. Place over boiling water and beat for about 7 minutes. Remove from boiling water. Add vanilla, and continue beating until glossy and spreadable.

14. Frost top and sides.

**PREPARATION TIME: 45 minutes including cooling**
**BAKING TIME: 30 minutes**

# BLUEBERRY CAKE WITH LEMON MERINGUE SAUCE

This cake is luscious served warm with Lemon Meringue Sauce spooned over each piece. It is a first rate reward after a morning of blueberry picking. Having fancied it for Mother's Day tea, I can attest to its being almost as delicious using frozen berries.

The cake can be prepared ahead, but save the sauce for the last minute.

| | |
|---|---|
| 2 | cups fresh blueberries |
| ¼ | cup butter |
| ½ | cup granulated sugar |
| 1 | egg |
| 1 | teaspoon vanilla extract |
| 1¾ | cups flour |
| 1½ | teaspoons baking powder |
| ½ | teaspoon salt |
| ⅓ | cup milk |
| ¼ | teaspoon cinnamon |

*Topping*

| | |
|---|---|
| 4 | tablespoons butter |
| ½ | cup granulated sugar |
| ½ | cup flour |

1. Preheat oven to 375 degrees.
2. Wash and drain blueberries in a sieve.
3. Cream ¼ cup butter and ½ cup sugar until light; beat in egg and vanilla.
4. In a smaller mixing bowl, combine flour, baking powder and salt.
5. Beginning and ending with the dry ingredients, alternately add flour mixture and milk to the creamed butter.
6. Mix to just blend.
7. Spoon batter into a greased 9-inch round cake pan. Smooth top.
8. Gently dry blueberries with a towel, and spread over the batter. Sprinkle with cinnamon.
9. To prepare topping, combine butter, sugar and flour with fingers until crumbly.
10. Sprinkle topping over berries.
11. Bake for 45 minutes.
12. Remove cake from oven and cool slightly on rack.
13. Serve warm with Lemon Meringue Sauce.

**YIELD: 8 servings**
**PREPARATION TIME: 20 minutes**
**BAKING TIME: 45 minutes**

# LEMON MERINGUE SAUCE

Although I sometimes substitute dried lemon peel, sold in small spice jars, nothing is like the real boost from fresh lemons. For zest, use only the thin yellow layer of rind; the white inner layer is bitter. A small tool, with four or five small holes, called a zester, is very handy and does a good job.

This sauce is excellent served over fresh berries, winter fruit salads, frozen desserts and cakes.

| | |
|---|---|
| 3 | egg yolks |
| ¾ | cup granulated sugar |
| ¼ | cup lemon juice |
| 1 | teaspoon grated lemon zest |
| 2 | egg whites |

1. Beat yolks until very light and thick.
2. Add half of the sugar (6 tablespoons) and continue beating until well mixed.
3. Stir in lemon juice and zest.
4. Transfer mixture to the top of a double boiler. Stir it over simmering water until sauce is thick and smooth, about 5 minutes.
5. Beat whites of 2 eggs. When they begin to foam, add remaining 6 tablespoons sugar and continue beating until soft peaks form.
6. Fold whites into lemon-yolk sauce thoroughly.
7. Serve in a crystal bowl, and ladle onto cake slices.

**YIELD: 2 cups**
**PREPARATION TIME: 25 minutes**

# PUMPKIN BREAD PUDDING

An enticing foray into a darker and spicier world, although not for bread pudding purists. Serve this with whiskey flavored hard sauce.

| | |
|---|---|
| 1 | tablespoon butter |
| ½ | loaf plus 2 slices pumpkin bread (see page 24) |
| 3 | cups warm milk |
| 3 | eggs |
| 4 | tablespoons granulated sugar |
| 1 | teaspoon vanilla extract |
| ¼ | teaspoon almond extract |
| 1 | tablespoon sugar |

1. Preheat oven to 350 degrees.
2. Spread 1 tablespoon butter in a casserole.
3. Set aside 2 slices of bread. Slice the ½ loaf into approximately ⅓-inch slices. Stack these and cut into about ¾-inch fingers. There should be about 4 cups, packed loosely. Reserve.
4. In a saucepan, heat the milk. Toss with the bread pieces. Let sit for 15 minutes.
5. In a separate bowl, combine eggs, 4 tablespoons sugar, and extracts. Beat well.
6. Combine bread and eggs together in the casserole. Stir all together with a wooden spoon.
7. Cut the remaining 2 slices of bread into quarters. Lay on top of pudding. Sprinkle with remaining 1 tablespoon sugar.
8. Bake for 1 hour or longer until a knife inserted comes out almost clean.
9. Spoon into small bowls. Add a spoonful of Whiskey Hard Sauce to top.

**YIELD: 8–10 servings**
**PREPARATION TIME: 20 minutes**
**BAKING TIME: 60–70 minutes**

# WHISKEY HARD SAUCE

4 tablespoons butter, room temperature

1 cup powdered sugar

1½ teaspoons bourbon or whiskey

1 teaspoon heavy cream (optional)

1. Cream the butter.
2. Gradually add the powdered sugar, continuing to cream until fluffy.
3. Stir in whiskey and cream.
4. Spread on a small plate in a mound about 1-inch high. Refrigerate.

YIELD: About ½ cup
PREPARATION TIME: 10 minutes

VARIATIONS: The hard sauce can be flavored with vanilla extract, orange rind and juice, or rum.

# POACHED APRICOTS WITH ALMOND WHIPPED CREAM

I had been operating under an unspoken "apricot" rule. In Vermont, fresh apricots are only available for a very short season, and, therefore, should be enjoyed to their utmost fullness, just as they are, eaten in hand. Cooking was for dried and canned apricots or preserves. Well . . . so goes rules. I think this dessert pays due respect to apricots . . . and then some.

An excellent example of simply elegant, this dessert is stunning, yet straight-forward. Serve on clear glass dishes, garnished perhaps with a green leaf. It can all be prepared in advance, except for the whipped cream, which is always better done just prior to serving.

| | |
|---|---|
| 4–6 | ripe apricots |
| ½ | cup granulated sugar |
| 1 | cup water |
| | Few drops lemon juice |
| ½ | teaspoon lemon peel |

*Topping*

| | |
|---|---|
| ¾ | cup heavy cream |
| 2–3 | tablespoons powdered sugar |
| ½ | teaspoon almond extract |

1. To peel apricots, drop into boiling water for one minute. Remove and set in cold water. Skins will slip off easily.
2. Combine sugar, water and lemon juice in a medium saucepan to make a poaching syrup. Boil syrup for 4 minutes.
3. Add apricots; reduce heat and simmer 5–7 minutes, until tender.
4. Remove apricots and chill in refrigerator. If you wish, halve apricots and remove pits. (I prefer to serve them whole.)
5. Reduce syrup to half, by boiling. Cool.
6. Whip heavy cream until frothy. Add sugar and extract. Continue whipping until cream is thickened but not stiff.
7. Put a spoonful of the reduced syrup in the bottom of pretty individual bowls or dessert plates. Place an apricot (or 2) on the syrup and top with a small amount of whipped cream (do not cover all of the apricot).

**YIELD: 4–6 servings (or 2–3 using 2 apricots per person)**
**PREPARATION TIME: under ½ hour**
**COOKING TIME: 8 minutes**

# PEARS IN CREME CARAMEL

Here is a good, simple, and comforting dessert. We would often make this for the children on Saturday nights, when we left them early with a sitter. Their dinners on those nights were very simple, soft boiled egg-and-toast sorts of meals, and this dessert made the meal somewhat special, or so I imagined.

| | |
|---|---|
| 4 | pears, peeled, cut in half (lengthwise) and cored |
| 4 | tablespoons granulated sugar |
| 1–2 | tablespoons butter, preferably unsalted |
| ²/₃ | cup heavy cream |
| ½ | teaspoon vanilla extract |

1. Preheat oven to 475 degrees.
2. Arrange pears, cut side down in a shallow buttered baking dish. They need to fit closely without much excess space.
3. Sprinkle pears with sugar. Dot with butter.
4. Bake 12 minutes, basting 2 or 3 times.
5. Mix cream and vanilla. Pour over all.
6. Stir and bake a few minutes more. Sugar will be nicely browned.

**YIELD: 4–8 servings**
**PREPARATION TIME: 10 minutes**
**BAKING TIME: 15 minutes**

# BETTY BACON'S FROSTED LAYER CAKE

An all-time favorite yellow cake with a dark and buttery chocolate icing. Betty Bacon was the best cook I knew when I was a child, and a true inspiration to me. I remember making all sorts of excuses to visit her after school to watch her cook, hoping for a cake and milk invitation. It's been many years since I've seen her, but this cake remains the ultimate comforting cake.

For better cakes, always have all cake ingredients as close to room temperature as possible. When preparing cake batters, the butter and sugar should be well creamed and the eggs well beaten. After the eggs are beaten, gently mix or fold in the remaining dry and liquid ingredients with a rubber spatula or wooden spoon. When adding wet and dry ingredients to the batter alternately, begin and end with the dry ingredients.

| | |
|---|---|
| ½ | cup butter, at room temperature |
| 1½ | cups granulated sugar |
| 3 | eggs |
| 2 | cups flour |
| 2 | teaspoons baking powder |
| | Pinch salt |
| 1 | cup milk |

1. Preheat the oven to 375 degrees.
2. Cream the butter. Gradually add the sugar, while continuing to cream until light and fluffy.
3. Add eggs, one at a time, beating well after each addition.
4. Sift dry ingredients together.
5. Alternately, blend the dry ingredients and the milk into the creamed butter.
6. Divide batter into 2 greased 8-inch cake pans.
7. Bake for 25 minutes.
8. Cool on a rack for 5 minutes, and turn out of pans.
9. When completely cool, frost.

**YIELD: 12 servings**
**PREPARATION TIME: 30 minutes**
**BAKING TIME: 25 minutes**

# FAVORITE CHOCOLATE ICING

| | |
|---|---|
| 4 | squares unsweetened chocolate |
| 2½ | cups powdered sugar |
| 1 | teaspoon vanilla extract |
| ¼ | cup water |
| 1 | egg |
| 6 | tablespoons butter, melted |

1. Melt chocolate in the top of a double boiler.

2. Remove saucepan from hot water. Add sugar, vanilla and water, beating until stiff.

3. Add egg and butter, mixing until smooth and spreadable.

4. Allow icing to set for a while, if it needs to thicken.

5. For ease in frosting, dip knife in hot water. Apply icing to the sides of the cake first, then frost the top. After joining top and sides, smooth sides with one final, even stroke.

YIELD: Frosting for top, middle, and sides of layer cake.
PREPARATION TIME: 5 minutes

# UPHILL FARM APPLE TART

This crust can be made ahead of time and refrigerated until just prior to adding the filling and baking. Bake in a 9-inch round pan—a springform or flan pan with a removable bottom works well. Calvados-flavored unsweetened whipped cream can be spooned alongside each serving.

| | |
|---|---|
| 1 | cup plus 2 tablespoons unbleached flour |
| ½ | teaspoon salt |
| 1 | teaspoon granulated sugar |
| 1 | teaspoon baking powder |
| ½ | cup butter or margarine |
| 1 | egg yolk |
| 2 | tablespoons Calvados, brandy or rum |
| 4 | apples, peeled, cored and cut in eighths |
| 2 | tablespoons sliced almonds |

*Topping*

| | |
|---|---|
| ½–⅔ | cup granulated sugar |
| 2 | tablespoons flour |
| ½ | teaspoon ground cinnamon |

1. Preheat oven to 350 degrees.
2. Combine dry ingredients.
3. Cut in butter, using 2 knives.
4. Add the egg yolk and Calvados. Combine with fingers.
5. Press dough into a 9-inch pan, bringing up sides to form an edge.
6. Arrange sliced apples in concentric circles or other pattern.
7. Sprinkle with almonds.
8. Make a topping, combining sugar, flour and cinnamon. Sprinkle over apples and almonds.
9. Bake for 45 minutes.
10. Remove to rack to cool.

YIELD: 8 servings
PREPARATION TIME: 30 minutes
BAKING TIME: 45 minutes

# DECEMBER'S CAKE

## (A Walnut Pound Cake)

I make and freeze many of these walnut pound cakes early in December, defrost and then glaze them as needed for holiday giving. I think they are prettiest baked in a 9-inch tube pan, but they also work well in a 9" x 5" x 3" loaf pan.

| | |
|---|---|
| 1½ | cups sifted flour |
| ¼ | teaspoon baking soda |
| 1¼ | cups granulated sugar |
| 1 | cup butter, room temperature |
| 1½ | tablespoons lemon juice |
| ½ | teaspoon almond extract |
| 1 | teaspoon vanilla extract |
| 5 | eggs, separated |
| 1 | cup coarsely chopped walnuts or pecans |
| ⅛ | teaspoon salt |
| 1 | teaspoon cream of tartar |

*Glaze*

| | |
|---|---|
| 1 | cup sifted powdered sugar |
| ½ | teaspoon vanilla extract |
| 1 | teaspoon milk |

1. Preheat oven to 325 degrees.
2. Butter and flour a 9-inch tube pan.
3. Mix flour, baking soda and ¾ cup granulated sugar into a bowl.
4. Add butter, and blend in with your fingers or a wooden spoon.
5. Add lemon juice and extracts. Mix in egg yolks one at a time blending well after each addition.
6. Fold in coarsely chopped nuts.
7. In a separate bowl, beat egg whites until stiff. Gradually add remaining granulated sugar, cream of tartar and salt to the stiff egg whites.
8. Fold egg whites into the nut batter until thoroughly incorporated.
9. Spoon into pan and spread evenly.
10. Bake for about 1 hour. Turn off heat and let cake remain in oven for an additional 10–15 minutes.
11. Invert on rack covered with waxed paper to cool.
12. When cool, wrap well to freeze, or make the following glaze to use now.
13. Add vanilla and milk to the sifted powdered sugar. Amounts are approximate and should be adjusted to make the glaze easy to spread.

**PREPARATION TIME: 30 minutes**
**BAKING TIME: 70 minutes**

# ANNIVERSARY COEUR À LA CREME

This recipe and the white porcelain heart-shaped mold needed to make it were wedding presents from Sheela Harden, great cook and manager of The Brasserie in Bennington, Vermont. Partly out of sentiment, partly because I really like the heart-shaped mold, and mostly because this is an absolutely wonderful recipe, we have continued to prepare it each year as an anniversary treat.

I have written the recipe as I received it, beating the cream in a copper bowl over ice. This is how I make it, but, however you usually whip heavy cream should be fine.

The heart-shaped mold is generally of white porcelain with holes in the bottom to drain the whey. It is an appealing looking kitchen tool which is readily available.

In case you've always wanted to buy one, here is all the justification you'll need.

You will also need cotton cheesecloth. Start the preparation the day before you will be serving it.

| | |
|---|---|
| 8 | ounces cream cheese, at room temperature |
| ½ | cup sifted powdered sugar |
| | Pinch salt |
| 1 | large vanilla bean |
| 1 | pint heavy cream |

1. Beat the cream cheese until light and fluffy.

2. Add the powdered sugar, salt and the inside scrapings of one vanilla bean. Beat until well mixed and light.

3. In a large copper bowl over ice, whip cream by hand with a large balloon whisk.

4. Fold cream cheese into the whipped cream. Mix well. Do not be afraid to be vigorous.

5. Line the mold with a double layer of cheesecloth that has been soaked in ice water and wrung out. Leave flaps large enough to cover top.

6. Fill the mold and cover the top with the cheesecloth flaps. Set mold on a dish to catch the whey and refrigerate overnight.

*Sauce*

| | |
|---|---|
| 1½ | cups red currant jelly |
| ⅓ | cup good dry sherry |
| 1 | pint strawberries or raspberries |
| | Splash Kirsch, optional |

7. To unmold: Unwrap cheesecloth and turn out on a serving dish. Lift off cheesecloth. Garnish with a few berries and serve with sauce.

8. For sauce: Melt red currant jelly with sherry. Stir until it all melts. Let cool, stirring occasionally. Add berries and optional Kirsch.

**YIELD: 1 heart mold**
**PREPARATION TIME: 25 minutes**
**REFRIGERATION TIME: Overnight**

# MOTHER'S RICE PUDDING

This is a creamy rice pudding. Rumor has it you need my mother's big yellow bowl to make it taste just right. I'm not convinced.

| | |
|---|---|
| 4 | cups milk |
| ⅔–1 | cup granulated sugar |
| 1 | tablespoon vanilla extract |
| ½ | cup raisins |
| ⅓–½ | cup cooked rice (I use brown rice) |
| 5 | eggs, beaten |

1. Preheat oven to 325 degrees.

2. Combine all of the ingredients in a medium-sized ovenproof serving bowl or casserole.

3. To bake, set bowl in a pan of water.

4. Bake for about 1 hour and 10 minutes, or until a knife inserted near center comes out clean.

**YIELD: 8–10 servings**
**PREPARATION TIME: 15 minutes**
**BAKING TIME: 75 minutes**

# LAURA'S BIRTHDAY TRIFLE

Although married to an enthusiastic dessert maker, Laura requests this trifle again and again for her birthday. It is a splendid use for rhubarb!

Don't let the preparation of trifle overwhelm you. Simply separate it into its three component parts: cake layers, fruit layers, and *crème anglaise*. Each can be made separately and in advance. The completed trifle needs at least 6 hours of refrigeration before serving. Trifle should be assembled in a deep, straight-sided glass bowl.

*Cake layers*

| | |
|---|---|
| 6 | **eggs, separated** |
| ⅔–¾ | **cup granulated sugar** |
| ¼ | **teaspoon vanilla or lemon extract** |
| 1½ | **cups minus 2 tablespoons flour** |
| | **Pinch salt** |

1. Preheat oven to 325 degrees. Grease an 8-inch springform pan.
2. Beat the egg yolks. Gradually add sugar and continue beating until light and fluffy. Stir in flavoring.
3. Gently fold flour into the yolk mixture.
4. In a separate bowl, beat egg whites and salt until just stiff. Fold ¼ of whites into the yolk-flour mixture to lighten it. Then fold in remaining whites.
5. Pour into the greased pan. Bake 45 minutes.
6. Let cool on wire rack. Wrap in plastic wrap until time to assemble.
7. When ready to assemble, split the cake into 4 thin layers, using a long sharp knife and a sawing motion.

*Fruit layer*

| | |
|---|---|
| 5–6 | **cups rhubarb, cut in 2-inch lengths** |
| ¾ | **cup granulated sugar** |
| ½ | **cup water** |

1. Combine rhubarb, sugar and water in a heavy-bottomed saucepan.
2. Bring to a boil; cover and simmer for 10 minutes.
3. Uncover and stir over moderate heat until most of the liquid is gone, about 10 minutes.
4. Let cool.

*Crème Anglaise*

**3** **cups** *Crème Anglaise* **(see page 118)**

**6** **tablespoons strawberry-rhubarb jam**

**Sherry (optional)**

1. Prepare according to recipe on page.
2. Cover and chill for at least an hour, until assembling trifle.

Assembly:

1. Sprinkle cut side of cake layers with sherry and spread each layer with 2 tablespoons preserves.
2. Build trifle in a deep serving dish about 8 inches in diameter. A glass dish is preferable. Spread first cake layer with ⅓ of the rhubarb and ½ cup of *crème anglaise*. Continue layering cake, fruit and custard sauce, ending with a cake layer. Pour remaining *crème anglaise* over top.
3. Refrigerate for at least 6 hours.

**YIELD: 8–10 servings**
**PREPARATION TIME: 1–1½ hours**
  **(can be done in stages)**
**REFRIGERATION TIME: 6-plus hours**

**VARIATIONS:** Variations are part of the fun of trifles. Many recipes call for ready-made sponge or pound cake, or lady fingers. These, of course, can be substituted for a time-saving, albeit a sacrifice in taste, too. The cake layers can be doused with sherry, Kirsch, rum or liqueurs for added flavor. Various jams can be used or can be omitted all together. I prefer strawberry-rhubarb with this recipe, but try ginger preserves for a zesty bite. Strawberry and plum jams also work well.

# HAZELNUT ROLL WITH CREAM FILLING

There are three parts to this dessert: the cake, baked in a jelly roll pan, whipped cream filling, and an apricot glaze. It really is not hard to make once you overcome any fear of rolling cakes. It's easy, you'll see, and spectacular.

You will need a 10½″ x 15½″ jelly roll pan to make this roulade. Butter the pan; then fit with waxed paper overhanging the sides. Butter the waxed paper also. When grinding the nuts, use a pulsing action to prevent making a nut butter or paste.

This cake can be made 1 day ahead and refrigerated overnight. Let stand at room temperature 20 minutes before serving. When serving, use a serrated knife in a sawing fashion to prevent crushing the cake.

*Cake*

| | |
|---|---|
| 6 | eggs, separated |
| ¾ | cup granulated sugar |
| 1½ | cups ground hazelnuts (or very finely chopped) |
| 1 | teaspoon baking powder |
| ⅛ | teaspoon salt |

*Glaze*

| | |
|---|---|
| 6 | tablespoons apricot preserves or jam |
| 2 | tablespoons brandy |

*Filling*

| | |
|---|---|
| 1¼ | cups heavy cream |
| 2 | tablespoons powdered sugar |
| 1–2 | tablespoons rum |

1. Preheat oven to 350 degrees. Butter jelly roll pan and fit with waxed paper overhanging sides.

2. Beat egg yolks until pale and thickened.

3. Beat in sugar until blended.

4. Combine ground hazelnuts and baking powder; stir into yolk mixture and set aside.

5. Beat egg whites, adding salt once they are foamy. Continue beating until stiff.

6. Gently stir a spoonful of egg whites into the yolk mixture. With a rubber spatula fold the remaining whites into the yolk mixture.

7. Spread batter into prepared pan. Smooth lightly.

8. Bake for approximately 15 minutes or until a cake tester comes out clean.

*Topping*
**4–6 whole hazelnuts**
**Powdered sugar**

9. Using the waxed paper, turn the cake out onto a clean dish towel. Remove the waxed paper. Trim any hard edges. Fold edge of dish towel over the long side of cake and roll cake lengthwise up in towel. Lift cake wrapped in towel onto a rack to cool.

10. Meanwhile prepare the glaze by melting the jam and brandy in a small pan.

11. To prepare the filling, whip the cream with powdered sugar and rum until stiff.

12. Unroll the cake, brush on the glaze. Let rest a few minutes.

13. Spread on the cream filling and roll the cake again.

14. Slide onto a serving board or platter, seam side down. Sift additional powdered sugar over top if desired and decorate with a few whole hazelnuts. Refrigerate until serving.

**YIELD: 10–12 servings**
**PREPARATION TIME: 45 minutes**
**BAKING TIME: 15 minutes**

**VARIATIONS:** After rolling the cake, pipe additional whipped cream into rosettes along the top of the cake. Put a whole hazelnut in the center of each rosette.
The glaze can be omitted and 2 tablespoons of hazelnut praline can be folded into the whipped cream.

# MAPLE FLOATING ISLANDS

This intriguing dessert with its equally intriguing name is an old favorite. It is as lovely looking as it sounds, white puffs floating on a sea of maple custard.

*Islands*

| 3 | egg whites |
|---|---|
|  | Pinch salt |
| 6 | tablespoons granulated sugar |

*Custard*

| 2 | cups milk (or ½ cream, ½ milk) |
|---|---|
| 6 | egg yolks |
| 4 | tablespoons pure maple syrup |
| 1 | teaspoon vanilla extract |

1. Begin by preparing the islands. Beat egg whites with salt until foamy. Gradually add sugar, beating until stiff.

2. Scald the milk in a shallow pan. Drop tablespoons of the island meringues onto the milk. Poach gently for about 2 minutes on each side. Remove them with a slotted spoon and drain on a towel.

3. In a heavy-bottomed saucepan, beat the egg yolks slightly. Add the maple syrup.

4. Slowly stir in the scalded milk. Cook over a very slow heat, stirring constantly, until the mixture begins to thicken and coats the back of a spoon. This will take between 5 and 10 minutes. Do not allow custard to boil. Cool and stir in vanilla.

5. Pour the custard in a shallow serving dish. Float the meringue islands on top. Chill until serving.

YIELD: 4–5 servings
PREPARATION TIME: 30 minutes
COOKING TIME: 15 minutes

# CHOCOLATE CHIP PECAN PIE

A very rich and gooey and delicious dessert—serve with unsweetened whipped cream.

| | |
|---|---|
| 1 | 9-inch pie crust, unbaked (see page 150) |
| 3 | eggs |
| 1¼ | cups granulated sugar |
| ½ | cup flour |
| 5 | tablespoons sweet butter, melted |
| 1¼ | cups semisweet chocolate bits |
| 1½ | cups chopped pecans |
| ½ | teaspoon salt |
| ½ | teaspoon vanilla extract |
| ½ | cup light corn syrup |

1. Preheat oven to 350 degrees.
2. Beat eggs well in a bowl.
3. Stir in remaining ingredients.
4. Pour into pastry shell.
5. Bake for 45 minutes.

YIELD: 10 servings
PREPARATION TIME: 15 minutes
BAKING TIME: 45 minutes

# MRS. WILSON'S CAKE

This is such an easy cake, made quickly from ingredients generally on hand. On those long-seeming, gray afternoons, this cake always gives the children a lift . . . and us also, we admit.

A mixing bowl for the cake, a bowl for the topping, and an 8-inch square pan are all you need. Or, if you wish, double this recipe and bake in an 11″ x 7″ pan. The topping here is quite sweet; the cake is excellent without any topping if you prefer.

| | |
|---|---|
| 1 | cup granulated sugar |
| 1½ | cups flour |
| 3 | tablespoons cocoa |
| ½ | teaspoon salt |
| 1 | teaspoon baking soda |
| 5 | tablespoons butter, melted |
| 1 | tablespoon cider vinegar |
| 1 | teaspoon vanilla extract |
| 1 | cup cold water |

*Topping*

| | |
|---|---|
| ½ | cup brown sugar |
| 3 | tablespoons butter, melted |
| 3 | tablespoons heavy cream |

1. Preheat oven to 400 degrees.
2. Sift sugar, flour, cocoa, salt, and baking soda into a bowl.
3. Make a well in the center, and add melted butter and the liquid ingredients.
4. Beat well.
5. Pour into an 8-inch square pan. Bake for 30 minutes. Cool completely before spreading topping. Turn oven off.
6. For topping, mix brown sugar, butter and heavy cream.
7. Spread over the cooled cake and set under broiler for 1 minute. Watch carefully to prevent burning.
8. Allow frosting to cool. Serve from pan.

YIELD: 12–16 pieces
PREPARATION TIME: 15 minutes
BAKING TIME: 30 minutes

# SOUR CREAM NUT CUPCAKES WITH MAPLE FROSTING

Delicate tasting little cakes that are a wonderful complement to the frosting which is neither too sweet nor sticky. It, too, is subtle and delicious.

*Cupcakes*

| | |
|---|---|
| ½ | cup butter (1 stick) |
| ¾ | cup granulated sugar |
| 2 | eggs |
| 1 | cup sour cream |
| ½ | teaspoon baking soda |
| 1 | tablespoon hot water |
| 1⅓ | cups flour |
| ¼ | teaspoon salt |
| 1 | teaspoon baking powder |
| ½ | cup chopped pecans |
| 1 | tablespoon vanilla extract |

*Frosting*

| | |
|---|---|
| 2 | tablespoons butter |
| 2 | cups powdered sugar |
| ¼ | teaspoon salt |
| 4 | tablespoons pure maple syrup |

1. Preheat oven to 375 degrees.
2. To prepare cupcakes, cream butter. Gradually add sugar, creaming until light.
3. Mix in eggs, beating well after each addition.
4. Add sour cream; stir well.
5. Dissolve baking soda in water. Mix in.
6. Sift flour with salt and baking powder.
7. Gradually fold sifted ingredients into the butter mixture. Add the pecans and the vanilla.
8. Grease and lightly flour cupcake tins.
9. Fill to ⅔-full.
10. Bake for 15–20 minutes.
11. Cool on racks.
12. To prepare frosting, cream butter. Sift powdered sugar and gradually add with salt to butter.
13. Stir in syrup; then beat until smooth and spreadable.
14. Frost well-cooled cupcakes.

YIELD: 12 cupcakes
PREPARATION TIME: 30 minutes
BAKING TIME: 20 minutes

# WASHINGTON'S BIRTHDAY PIE

Every year our children act out their own version of "Little George's" cherry tree incident. And every year we end the play with applause and this pie. The first year, we had a pretty shy little George. He never quite got past chopping the tree down, repeatedly knocking it over and, setting it back up again. Despite his single-minded performance, he did understand the point. During dessert, he looked up and said, in all candor, "Mom. I can not tell a lie; I hate this cherry pie."

*Some* of us love it.

| | |
|---|---|
| 1 | 9-inch double pastry crust, unbaked (see page 150) |
| 1½ | pounds (4 cups) fresh, pitted, sour red cherries or 3 cups canned water-packed sour red cherries, drained and liquid reserved |
| 1⅓ | cups granulated sugar |
| 4 | tablespoons flour |
| ⅛ | teaspoon salt |
| ¼ | teaspoon almond extract |
| ⅓ | cup water (or liquid from drained canned cherries) |
| 2 | tablespoons butter |
| | Milk and sugar (optional) |

1. Preheat oven to 425 degrees.
2. Combine sugar, flour, salt, extract, liquid, and mix with the cherries.
3. Roll out pastry. Place half in a 9-inch pie tin.
4. Pour in cherry mixture. Dot with butter. Cut and trim bottom crust to have about a 1-inch overhang.
5. Roll remaining ½ pastry and cut into ½-inch strips. Weave strips in a lattice over pie. Seal edges.
6. The lattice can be brushed with milk and sprinkled with sugar.
7. Bake for 10 minutes; reduce heat to 350 degrees and continue baking for 30 minutes more.

Tip: This is a bubbly pie. Put a baking sheet on a lower oven shelf to catch spills.

YIELD: 8 servings
PREPARATION TIME: 30 minutes
BAKING TIME: 40 minutes

**VARIATION:** 3 tablespoons of tapioca or 3 tablespoons cornstarch can substitute for 4 tablespoons flour.

# MOCHA FUDGE TART

An unbaked fudgey temptation. Make it once, and see if you aren't tempted to make it again and again. It is very easy to prepare, but start in early enough as it requires several hours of refrigeration.

*Crust*

| | |
|---|---|
| 1⅓ | cups chocolate wafer cookie crumbs |
| 6 | tablespoons unsalted butter, melted |

*Filling*

| | |
|---|---|
| 1 | cup granulated sugar |
| 2 | tablespoons flour |
| ⅛ | teaspoon salt |
| ¼ | cup heavy cream |
| 2 | eggs, at room temperature |
| 1 | tablespoon instant coffee powder |
| 1 | cup boiling water |
| 2 | ounces unsweetened chocolate |
| 4 | tablespoons unsalted butter |
| 1 | teaspoon vanilla extract |

*Topping*

| | |
|---|---|
| ⅔ | cup heavy cream |
| 1 | tablespoon powdered sugar |
| ½ | teaspoon vanilla extract |
| | Semisweet chocolate for grating |

1. Lightly grease an 8-inch springform pan.
2. Combine cookie crumbs and 6 tablespoons melted butter. Press crust on the bottom and about 2 inches up the sides of the pan.
3. Refrigerate crust for at least ½ hour.
4. Meanwhile, prepare filling in a heavy-bottomed saucepan. Mix the sugar, flour, and salt in the saucepan. Stir in the cream and eggs.
5. Mix the coffee in the boiling water.
6. Place the saucepan over low heat. Gradually pour in the boiling coffee, stirring constantly.
7. Continue stirring until filling comes to a boil. Stir and boil for 1 minute.
8. Remove from heat. Stir in the chocolate and the butter.
9. Set the pan in a bowl, partially filled with ice water. Beat the mixture. When it cools somewhat, add vanilla. Continue beating until thick, glossy, and lukewarm.
10. Spoon filling into the crumb crust, and refrigerate for about 4 hours or until firm.
11. To prepare the topping, beat the cream with the sugar and vanilla until soft peaks form.
12. Either mound the cream on top of the tart, or serve it in a bowl, spooning some alongside each slice when serving.
13. Grate chocolate on top of cream.

YIELD: 8–10 servings
PREPARATION TIME: 30 minutes
REFRIGERATION TIME: 4 hours

# OUR BÛCHE DE NÖEL

## A Chocolate Roll With A Chestnut Cream Filling

Apart from all the tinsel and glitter of Christmas is our yule log sitting on a wooden platter surrounded by fir boughs, on the sideboard.

As the lights and excitement of the day dim, after the spirited dinner has been shared, we take pause for one of my favorite moments. We gather, quietly, each reflecting on the day, the affections, the generosities.

And, in the candles' last glow, we share the yule log—a symbol of the extraordinary disguised as the ordinary—and feel the peace and interconnectedness of all in nature.

*Chocolate roll*

| | |
|---|---|
| 4 | eggs, separated |
| 3 | tablespoons cocoa |
| ¼ | cup flour |
| ¾ | cup granulated sugar |
| ½ | teaspoon vanilla extract |
| | Pinch salt |

*Filling*

| | |
|---|---|
| 1¾ | cups heavy cream |
| ½ | cup sweetened chestnut puree |
| 2 | tablespoons rum |
| 2 | tablespoons powdered sugar (or less to taste) |

1. Preheat oven to 325 degrees. Grease a 10½" x 15½" x 1" jelly roll pan. Line with waxed paper that overhangs the pan's edges. Grease and flour the waxed paper.

2. Mix together flour and cocoa. Set aside.

3. Beat egg yolks for 4–5 minutes, until thick. Gradually add half the sugar (6 tablespoons) and continue beating. Add vanilla and beat 4 more minutes, until thick.

4. Gently fold cocoa and flour mixture into the yolks.

5. Add a pinch of salt to egg whites in a separate bowl. With clean beaters, beat until foamy. Gradually add the remaining sugar and beat at high speed, until stiff and glossy.

6. With the rubber spatula, fold ¼ of the egg whites into the chocolate-yolk mixture.

7. Then, carefully fold the chocolate mixture into the remaining egg whites.

8. Pour the batter into the prepared pan; smooth evenly. Bake 20 minutes or until top springs back when lightly touched.

*Frosting*

**¾**   **cup semisweet chocolate pieces**

**3**   **tablespoons unsalted butter**

**1**   **tablespoon cream**

9. Turn cake out onto a slightly damp dish towel. Peel off waxed paper. Trim any hard edges. Roll up, starting from a long side with the towel. Let rolled cake cool on a rack.

10. To prepare cream filling: Whip cream until soft peaks form. Beat in chestnut puree, rum and sugar, to taste. Continue beating until stiff peaks form.

11. Carefully unroll the cake. Spread with the chestnut cream. Reroll the cake, using the towel to help lift it. Slide it, seam side down onto a wooden platter, long basket, or serving dish.

12. To prepare frosting: In top of a double boiler, over hot but not boiling water, melt chocolate and butter with the cream. Stir until smooth. Let set for a few minutes.

13. Quickly spread the frosting over the roll. Run the tines of a fork along the roll to resemble bark.

14. Adorn as you wish, perhaps with almond paste mushrooms or a dusting of powdered sugar to resemble snow.

15. To serve, slice with a serrated knife in a sawing motion in order not to crush the log.

**PREPARATION TIME: 50 minutes**
**BAKING TIME: 20 minutes**

# SOUR CREAM FUDGE FROSTING

I recently received a call from across the country, a woman friend requesting this frosting for her husband's 40th birthday cake. He had it at our home years ago, and raves about it still.

Try it on any yellow or chocolate cake. It should make a good cake, unforgettable.

| | |
|---|---|
| 2 | cups granulated sugar |
| ½ | cup sour cream |
| 2 | tablespoons cocoa |
| ½ | cup butter |
| ½ | teaspoon vanilla extract |
| | Pecan or walnut halves |

1. Combine all ingredients except vanilla and nuts in a heavy-bottomed saucepan.
2. Cook over medium heat until mixture just begins to bubble.
3. Lower heat, and cook for 2 minutes, stirring with a wooden spoon.
4. Remove from heat and set in cold water for 2 minutes. Stir in vanilla.
5. Remove from water and beat to a spreadable consistency. It will be somewhat loose as this icing sets on the cake.
6. Spoon between layers, on top, and on sides of an 8- or 9-inch layer cake.
7. Decorate with pecan or walnut halves.

**YIELD:** Frosting for top, middle, and sides of a 9-inch cake
**PREPARATION TIME:** 10 minutes

# CHOCOLATE BON-BONS

These are chocolate-covered ice cream balls. When I was a child, we bought them every Saturday afternoon at the matinee. I never see them at the movies anymore and although that distant taste memory has faded, I suspect this homemade version is infinitely better.

Place each bon-bon in a paper candy liner, as used for chocolates. Pass in a special candy dish when serving coffee and liqueurs.

| | |
|---|---|
| 1 | pint *good* ice cream, vanilla or coffee or . . . |
| 8 | ounces bittersweet or semisweet chocolate |
| 1 | tablespoon prepared coffee |

1. Shape the ice cream into balls, 1½ inches in diameter.
2. Freeze the balls for at least 3 hours or overnight in a foil-covered dish.
3. Line a shallow freezer container or dish with waxed paper.
4. Melt chocolate with coffee in a small deep pan.
5. Lift each ice cream ball with a toothpick and dip into the melted chocolate. Place on waxed paper. Work quickly, coating each ball with chocolate.
6. Cover the bon-bons with foil and freeze until serving time.

YIELD: 12 medium-sized bon-bons
PREPARATION TIME: 30 minutes
REFRIGERATION TIME: 3 hours or overnight

# BASIC PASTRIES

There are many versions of "short crusts" with variations in the fat used being the primary difference. Traditional cooks wouldn't think of using anything but lard; others prefer the ease of vegetable shortening. I, loving the flavor butter imparts, use butter cutting it with lard, shortening or margarine. The resulting pastry is certainly lighter than an all-butter crust, yet it's as delicious as only butter can make it.

As with all pastry, keep both the shortening and the water cold. Light handling keeps the pastry from being warmed by your hands.

## I. BASIC PIE CRUST

| | |
|---|---|
| 2 | cups flour |
| ½ | teaspoon salt |
| ⅓ | cup chilled butter |
| ⅓ | cup shortening (lard, vegetable shortening, margarine) |
| 4 | tablespoons ice water |

1. Combine flour and salt.
2. With 2 knives, cut in shortenings until mixture resembles coarse cornmeal.
3. While tossing the pastry with a fork, sprinkle it with ice water, a bit at a time. Continue tossing to moisten evenly.
4. Form pastry quickly into two pieces and chill for ½ hour before rolling out.
5. Continue according to the recipe of your choice.

**YIELD: 2 9-inch crusts or 1 double crust**
**PREPARATION TIME: 10 minutes**

---

**VARIATION:** For whole wheat pastry, use whatever proportion whole wheat flour to white flour you prefer, up to the total 2 cups flour called for. Be sure to sift the whole wheat flour to separate out any bran, husk or solids. Reserve these solids to enrich other foods.

# II. SOUR CREAM PASTRY

1½ cups unbleached white flour

½ pound butter, chilled (2 sticks)

½ cup sour cream

1. Using two knives or a pastry blender, cut the butter into the flour. The resulting mixture will look like coarse crumbs.

2. Stir in sour cream.

3. In a bowl, lightly knead pastry until it just holds its shape.

4. Wrap in plastic wrap and refrigerate a few hours or overnight.

5. Continue on with recipe of your choice.

YIELD: 1 pie crust
PREPARATION TIME: 10 minutes
REFRIGERATION TIME: 3 hours or overnight

# FROSTED ORANGE COW COOKIES

I quickly tire of plain sugar cookies yet I adore cookie cutters. A full platter of geese, teddy bears, or hearts is so appealing. I have a very favorite cow cookie cutter. We make lots, frosted white with orange spots, and hang them as ornaments on the Christmas tree for visitors to both nibble and bring home.

This cookie cutter recipe is more interesting than most—both the cookie and frosting have orange in them. But be sure to decorate them as plain cookies are only half the fun!

*Cookies*

| | |
|---|---|
| ½ | cup butter |
| ⅔ | cup granulated sugar |
| 1 | egg |
| 1 | tablespoon orange juice |
| 1–2 | teaspoons grated lemon rind |
| 2½ | cups flour |
| 1 | teaspoon baking powder |
| ¼ | teaspoon salt |

Cookies:

1. Cream butter and sugar in a large bowl until light and fluffy.
2. Beat in egg, orange juice and lemon rind.
3. Sift together dry ingredients.
4. Gradually stir dry ingredients into creamed mixture.
5. Gather the dough into a ball and wrap in plastic wrap. Refrigerate several hours or overnight.
6. Preheat oven to 350 degrees.
7. Roll out half of the dough on a lightly floured surface to ⅛-inch thickness.
8. Cut with a cookie cutter that has first been dipped in flour.
9. Place cookies on lightly greased baking sheets.
10. Repeat until all dough is used.
11. Bake a single sheet at a time for 8 minutes or until the edges are lightly browned. The cookies should remain pale.
12. Remove cookies from sheet and cool on wire rack.

*Frosting*

| 2 | egg whites |
|---|---|
| 2½–3 | cups powdered sugar |
| 1 | tablespoon orange juice, half diluted with water |
| | Food coloring (optional) |

Frosting:

1. Beat egg whites until foamy.
2. Gradually add sugar, beating until thick and creamy.
3. Add 1 tablespoon liquid slowly, stirring until frosting is the consistency you want.
4. Reserve some white frosting. Separate some to color. Decorate cookies.

YIELD: approximately 3 dozen
PREPARATION TIME: 30 minutes
REFRIGERATION TIME: 2 hours or more
BAKING TIME: 8 minutes

# A MIDSUMMER NIGHT'S PUNCH

Have a bash to celebrate midsummer's day, June 24th! Serve this punch in a large glass bowl with flowers afloat or with garlands of daisies and red clover surrounding it.

Make blocks of ice in milk cartons, freezing berries and blossoms within each block.

String tiny white lights out-of-doors, in the woods, if possible. Have players appear among the trees, reciting lines from *A Midsummer Night's Dream*.

Dance. Party. Cheer. Beckon the summertime.

| | |
|---|---|
| 1 | quart bottle white grape juice |
| 1 | quart bottle grapefruit juice |
| ½–1 | bottle dry white wine |
| | Green seedless grapes |
| | Strawberries |
| | Kiwi slices |
| | Honeydew melon balls |

1. Combine liquids.
2. Decorate with ice, fruits, flowers.

YIELD: 2½ quarts
PREPARATION TIME: 15 minutes

**VARIATIONS:** Make this an all-white punch, using white and light-green fruits, and white flowers.
Omit the wine, serve a plain punch, in the field or on the porch; it is pretty and refreshing.

# Index

salmon, cold poached, with watercress mayonnaise, 68–69

stew, Narrows, 72–73

Floating islands, maple, 140

Frosted layer cake, Betty Bacon's, 130–31

Frosted orange cow cookies, 152–53

Frosting
favorite chocolate icing, 131
sour cream fudge, 148

Fruit bowl, winter, 112

Fudge frosting, sour cream, 148

Fudge tart, mocha, 145

# G

Galaxy of onions, 100

Garlic soup au gratin, baked red onion and, 37

Garnishes, 58

Gazpacho salad, molded, 110

Ginger chicken, skewered, 82

Glazed tenderloin with sauce Cassis, 62–63

Golden potato puree, 101

Gougère with artichoke hearts and feta cheese, 60–61

Green bean(s)
and new potato salad, 109
potatoes and cornmeal dumplings, 49

# H

Ham
potatoes au gratin with leeks and, 39
in tarragon cream sauce, 33

Hard sauce, whiskey, 127

Hazelnut roll with cream filling, 138–39

Herbed artichoke sauce, linguine in, 81

Herbed croutons, 91
Vermont cheese soup with, 90–91

Herbs, 107

Hollandaise sauce, 67
chicken and puree of broccoli with, 66–67

Honey-soy vinaigrette, 105

Hot stuffed Italian bread, 45

Hungarian rice salad, 108

# I

Ice cream
chocolate bon-bons, 149

Icing
chocolate, favorite, 131
sour cream fudge frosting, 148

In-the-bowl dressing, 104

# L

Lamb
babootie, 48
cassoulet, New England, 30–31
and zucchini stew with lemon sauce, 42

Laura's birthday trifle, 136–37

Leeks
cold braised, in crème fraîche, 98–99
and ham, potatoes au gratin with, 39

Lemon
cream, luscious, 117
dijon dressing, 106
meringue sauce, 125
blueberry cake with, 124–25
pancake, Lookout, 21
roasted chicken, 84–85
sauce, lamb and zucchini stew with, 42
sauce, seafood rolls with, 64–65

Lemonade, strawberry, 116

Lentil and brown rice salad, 53

Leona's tourtiere, 46

Linguine in herbed artichoke sauce, 81

Lookout lemon pancake, 21

Louisiana sauce, baked red snapper in, 70–71

Lunch, spring, 88

Luscious lemon cream, 117

# M

Main dishes
babootie, 48
baked red snapper in Louisiana sauce, 70–71
barbecued chutney chicken, 50
basil chicken, 86
beef stew Provencal, 36
chicken and puree of broccoli with Hollandaise sauce, 66–67
chicken Marsala with proscuitini, 80
chicken plaza pie, 32
cold poached salmon with watercress mayonnaise, 68–69
country pork supper, 40–41
crumbed chicken in wine sauce, 78
glazed tenderloin with sauce Cassis, 62–63
gougère with artichoke hearts and feta cheese, 60–61
green beans, potatoes and cornmeal dumplings, 49
ham in tarragon cream sauce, 33
hot stuffed Italian bread, 45
lamb and zucchini stew with lemon sauce, 42
lemon roasted chicken, 84–85
lentil and brown rice salad, 53
Leona's tourtiere, 46
linguine in herbed artichoke sauce, 81
Maryland crab stew, 83
Narrows fish stew, 72–73
New England cassoulet, 30–31

# Other Quality Cookbooks

**DINING ON DECK:** Fine Food for Sailing & Boating
*by Linda Vail*

For Linda Vail a perfect day's sail includes fine food—quickly and easily prepared. She offers here 225 outstanding recipes (casual yet elegant food) with over 90 menus for everything from elegant weekends to hearty breakfasts and suppers for cool weather sailing. Her recipes are so good and so varied you'll use her cookbook year-round for sure!

160 pages, 8x10, illustrated.
Quality paperback, $10.95

---

**GOLDE'S HOMEMADE COOKIES**
*by Golde Hoffman Soloway*

"Cookies are her chosen realm and how sweet a world it is to visit."
Publishers Weekly

Over 100 treasured recipes that defy description. Suffice it to say that no one could walk away from Golde's cookies without asking for another . . . plus the recipe.

144 pages, 8¼x7¼, illustrations.
Quality paperback, $7.95

---

**SUMMER IN A JAR:** Making Pickles, Jams & More
*by Andrea Chesman*

"With recipes this simple and varied, it's hard to find an excuse not to preserve summer in one's cupboard."
Publishers Weekly

Chesman introduces single jar recipes so you can make pickles and relishes a single quart at a time. Plenty of low-sugar jams, marmalades, relishes. Pickles by the crock, too. Outstanding recipes.

160 pages, 8¼x7¼, illustrations.
Quality paperback, $7.95

---

*To order:*

At your bookstore or order directly from Williamson Publishing. Send check or money order to **Williamson Publishing Co., Church Hill Road, P.O. Box 185, Charlotte, Vermont 05445.** Please add $1.25 for postage and handling. Satisfaction guaranteed or full refund without question or quibble.

 **WILLIAMSON PUBLISHING**
CHARLOTTE, VERMONT 05445